ISBN 0-8373-0766-X

C-766 CAREER EXAMINATION SERIES

This is your PASSBOOK® for...

Stenographer

Test Preparation Study Guide

Questions & Answers

NATIONAL LEARNING CORPORATION

National Learning Corporation

212 Michael Drive, Syosset, New York 11791

(516) 921-8888
(800) 645-6337
FAX: (516) 921-8743
www.passbooks.com
sales @ passbooks.com
info @ passbooks.com

PRINTED IN THE UNITED STATES OF AMERICA

PASSBOOK®

NOTICE

This book is SOLELY intended for, is sold ONLY to, and its use is RESTRICTED to *individual*, bona fide applicants or candidates who qualify by virtue of having seriously filed applications for appropriate license, certificate, professional and/or promotional advancement, higher school matriculation, scholarship, or other legitimate requirements of educational and/or governmental authorities.

This book is NOT intended for use, class instruction, tutoring, training, duplication, copying, reprinting, excerption, or adaptation, etc., by:

(1) Other publishers

(2) Proprietors and/or Instructors of "Coaching" and/or Preparatory Courses

(3) Personnel and/or Training Divisions of commercial, industrial, and governmental organizations

(4) Schools, colleges, or universities and/or their departments and staffs, including teachers and other personnel

(5) Testing Agencies or Bureaus

(6) Study groups which seek by the purchase of a single volume to copy and/or duplicate and/or adapt this material for use by the group as a whole without having purchased individual volumes for each of the members of the group

(7) Et al.

Such persons would be in violation of appropriate Federal and State statutes.

PROVISION OF LICENSING AGREEMENTS. — Recognized educational commercial, industrial, and governmental institutions and organizations, and others legitimately engaged in educational pursuits, including training, testing, and measurement activities, may address a request for a licensing agreement to the copyright owners, who will determine whether, and under what conditions, including fees and charges, the materials in this book may be used by them. In other words, a licensing facility exists for the legitimate use of the material in this book on other than an individual basis. However, it is asseverated and affirmed here that the material in this book *CANNOT* be used without the receipt of the express permission of such a licensing agreement from the Publishers.

NATIONAL LEARNING CORPORATION
212 Michael Drive
Syosset, New York 11791

Inquiries re licensing agreements should be addressed to:
The President
National Learning Corporation
212 Michael Drive
Syosset, New York 11791

PASSBOOK® SERIES

THE *PASSBOOK® SERIES* has been created to prepare applicants and candidates for the ultimate academic battlefield – the examination room.

At some time in our lives, each and every one of us may be required to take an examination – for validation, matriculation, admission, qualification, registration, certification, or licensure.

Based on the assumption that every applicant or candidate has met the basic formal educational standards, has taken the required number of courses, and read the necessary texts, the *PASSBOOK® SERIES* furnishes the one special preparation which may assure passing with confidence, instead of failing with insecurity. Examination questions – together with answers – are furnished as the basic vehicle for study so that the mysteries of the examination and its compounding difficulties may be eliminated or diminished by a sure method.

This book is meant to help you pass your examination provided that you qualify and are serious in your objective.

The entire field is reviewed through the huge store of content information which is succinctly presented through a provocative and challenging approach – the question-and-answer method.

A climate of success is established by furnishing the correct answers at the end of each test.

You soon learn to recognize types of questions, forms of questions, and patterns of questioning. You may even begin to anticipate expected outcomes.

You perceive that many questions are repeated or adapted so that you can gain acute insights, which may enable you to score many sure points.

You learn how to confront new questions, or types of questions, and to attack them confidently and work out the correct answers.

You note objectives and emphases, and recognize pitfalls and dangers, so that you may make positive educational adjustments.

Moreover, you are kept fully informed in relation to new concepts, methods, practices, and directions in the field.

You discover that you are actually taking the examination all the time: you are preparing for the examination by "taking" an examination, not by reading extraneous and/or supererogatory textbooks.

In short, this PASSBOOK®, used directedly, should be an important factor in helping you to pass your test.

STENOGRAPHER

DUTIES;

Under direct supervision, with little latitude for independent or unreviewed action or decision, performs stenographic and related clerical duties of ordinary difficulty and responsibility; performs related work.

EXAMPLES OF TYPICAL TASKS

Takes dictation of ordinary difficulty and transcribes the dictation of routine correspondence, reports, and memoranda; may transcribe from a dictating machine; types copies, forms, schedules, charts and tables; performs a variety of miscellaneous routine clerical duties, such as searching files, filing, sorting mail, answering and relaying telephone messages; acts as receptionist; may operate office machines; relieves secretaries of routine duties.

SCOPE OF THE EXAMINATION

The written test will be designed to cover knowledges, skills, and/or abilities in the following areas:

1. Clerical aptitude;
2. Spelling; and
3. Alphabetizing.

HOW TO TAKE A TEST

I. YOU MUST PASS AN EXAMINATION

A. WHAT EVERY CANDIDATE SHOULD KNOW

Examination applicants often ask us for help in preparing for the written test. What can I study in advance? What kinds of questions will be asked? How will the test be given? How will the papers be graded?

As an applicant for a civil service examination, you may be wondering about some of these things. Our purpose here is to suggest effective methods of advance study and to describe civil service examinations.

Your chances for success on this examination can be increased if you know how to prepare. Those "pre-examination jitters" can be reduced if you know what to expect. You can even experience an adventure in good citizenship if you know why civil service exams are given.

B. WHY ARE CIVIL SERVICE EXAMINATIONS GIVEN?

Civil service examinations are important to you in two ways. As a citizen, you want public jobs filled by employees who know how to do their work. As a job seeker, you want a fair chance to compete for that job on an equal footing with other candidates. The best-known means of accomplishing this two-fold goal is the competitive examination.

Exams are widely publicized throughout the nation. They may be administered for jobs in federal, state, city, municipal, town or village governments or agencies.

Any citizen may apply, with some limitations, such as the age or residence of applicants. Your experience and education may be reviewed to see whether you meet the requirements for the particular examination. When these requirements exist, they are reasonable and applied consistently to all applicants. Thus, a competitive examination may cause you some uneasiness now, but it is your privilege and safeguard.

C. HOW ARE CIVIL SERVICE EXAMS DEVELOPED?

Examinations are carefully written by trained technicians who are specialists in the field known as "psychological measurement," in consultation with recognized authorities in the field of work that the test will cover. These experts recommend the subject matter areas or skills to be tested; only those knowledges or skills important to your success on the job are included. The most reliable books and source materials available are used as references. Together, the experts and technicians judge the difficulty level of the questions.

Test technicians know how to phrase questions so that the problem is clearly stated. Their ethics do not permit "trick" or "catch" questions. Questions may have been tried out on sample groups, or subjected to statistical analysis, to determine their usefulness.

Written tests are often used in combination with performance tests, ratings of training and experience, and oral interviews. All of these measures combine to form the best-known means of finding the right person for the right job.

II. HOW TO PASS THE WRITTEN TEST

A. NATURE OF THE EXAMINATION

To prepare intelligently for civil service examinations, you should know how they differ from school examinations you have taken. In school you were assigned certain definite pages to read or subjects to cover. The examination questions were quite detailed and usually emphasized memory. Civil service exams, on the other hand, try to discover your present ability to perform the duties of a position, plus your potentiality to learn these duties. In other words, a civil service exam attempts to predict how successful you will be. Questions cover such a broad area that they cannot be as minute and detailed as school exam questions.

In the public service similar kinds of work, or positions, are grouped together in one "class." This process is known as *position-classification.* All the positions in a class are paid according to the salary range for that class. One class title covers all of these positions, and they are all tested by the same examination.

B. FOUR BASIC STEPS

1) Study the announcement

How, then, can you know what subjects to study? Our best answer is: "Learn as much as possible about the class of positions for which you've applied." The exam will test the knowledge, skills and abilities needed to do the work.

Your most valuable source of information about the position you want is the official exam announcement. This announcement lists the training and experience qualifications. Check these standards and apply only if you come reasonably close to meeting them.

The brief description of the position in the examination announcement offers some clues to the subjects which will be tested. Think about the job itself. Review the duties in your mind. Can you perform them, or are there some in which you are rusty? Fill in the blank spots in your preparation.

Many jurisdictions preview the written test in the exam announcement by including a section called "Knowledge and Abilities Required," "Scope of the Examination," or some similar heading. Here you will find out specifically what fields will be tested.

2) Review your own background

Once you learn in general what the position is all about, and what you need to know to do the work, ask yourself which subjects you already know fairly well and which need improvement. You may wonder whether to concentrate on improving your strong areas or on building some background in your fields of weakness. When the announcement has specified "some knowledge" or "considerable knowledge," or has used adjectives like "beginning principles of..." or "advanced ... methods," you can get a clue as to the number and difficulty of questions to be asked in any given field. More questions, and hence broader coverage, would be included for those subjects which are more important in the work. Now weigh your strengths and weaknesses against the job requirements and prepare accordingly.

3) Determine the level of the position

Another way to tell how intensively you should prepare is to understand the level of the job for which you are applying. Is it the entering level? In other words, is this the position in which beginners in a field of work are hired? Or is it an intermediate or advanced level? Sometimes this is indicated by such words as "Junior" or "Senior" in the class title. Other jurisdictions use Roman numerals to designate the level – Clerk I, Clerk II, for example. The word "Supervisor" sometimes appears in the title. If the level is not indicated by the title, check the description of duties. Will you be working under very close supervision, or will you have responsibility for independent decisions in this work?

4) Choose appropriate study materials

Now that you know the subjects to be examined and the relative amount of each subject to be covered, you can choose suitable study materials. For beginning level jobs, or even advanced ones, if you have a pronounced weakness in some aspect of your training, read a modern, standard textbook in that field. Be sure it is up to date and has general coverage. Such books are normally available at your library, and the librarian will be glad to help you locate one. For entry-level positions, questions of appropriate difficulty are chosen – neither highly advanced questions, nor those too simple. Such questions require careful thought but not advanced training.

If the position for which you are applying is technical or advanced, you will read more advanced, specialized material. If you are already familiar with the basic principles of your field, elementary textbooks would waste your time. Concentrate on advanced textbooks and technical periodicals. Think through the concepts and review difficult problems in your field.

These are all general sources. You can get more ideas on your own initiative, following these leads. For example, training manuals and publications of the government agency which employs workers in your field can be useful, particularly for technical and professional positions. A letter or visit to the government department involved may result in more specific study suggestions, and certainly will provide you with a more definite idea of the exact nature of the position you are seeking.

III. KINDS OF TESTS

Tests are used for purposes other than measuring knowledge and ability to perform specified duties. For some positions, it is equally important to test ability to make adjustments to new situations or to profit from training. In others, basic mental abilities not dependent on information are essential. Questions which test these things may not appear as pertinent to the duties of the position as those which test for knowledge and information. Yet they are often highly important parts of a fair examination. For very general questions, it is almost impossible to help you direct your study efforts. What we can do is to point out some of the more common of these general abilities needed in public service positions and describe some typical questions.

1) General information

Broad, general information has been found useful for predicting job success in some kinds of work. This is tested in a variety of ways, from vocabulary lists to questions about current events. Basic background in some field of work, such as sociology or economics, may be sampled in a group of questions. Often these are principles which have become familiar to most persons through exposure rather than through formal training. It is difficult to advise you how to study for these questions; being alert to the world around you is our best suggestion.

2) Verbal ability

An example of an ability needed in many positions is verbal or language ability. Verbal ability is, in brief, the ability to use and understand words. Vocabulary and grammar tests are typical measures of this ability. Reading comprehension or paragraph interpretation questions are common in many kinds of civil service tests. You are given a paragraph of written material and asked to find its central meaning.

3) Numerical ability

Number skills can be tested by the familiar arithmetic problem, by checking paired lists of numbers to see which are alike and which are different, or by interpreting charts and graphs. In the latter test, a graph may be printed in the test booklet which you are asked to use as the basis for answering questions.

4) Observation

A popular test for law-enforcement positions is the observation test. A picture is shown to you for several minutes, then taken away. Questions about the picture test your ability to observe both details and larger elements.

5) Following directions

In many positions in the public service, the employee must be able to carry out written instructions dependably and accurately. You may be given a chart with several columns, each column listing a variety of information. The questions require you to carry out directions involving the information given in the chart.

6) Skills and aptitudes

Performance tests effectively measure some manual skills and aptitudes. When the skill is one in which you are trained, such as typing or shorthand, you can practice. These tests are often very much like those given in business school or high school courses. For many of the other skills and aptitudes, however, no short-time preparation can be made. Skills and abilities natural to you or that you have developed throughout your lifetime are being tested.

Many of the general questions just described provide all the data needed to answer the questions and ask you to use your reasoning ability to find the answers. Your best preparation for these tests, as well as for tests of facts and ideas, is to be at your physical and mental best. You, no doubt, have your own methods of getting into an exam-taking mood and keeping "in shape." The next section lists some ideas on this subject.

IV. KINDS OF QUESTIONS

Only rarely is the "essay" question, which you answer in narrative form, used in civil service tests. Civil service tests are usually of the short-answer type. Full instructions for answering these questions will be given to you at the examination. But in case this is your first experience with short-answer questions and separate answer sheets, here is what you need to know:

1) Multiple-choice Questions

Most popular of the short-answer questions is the "multiple choice" or "best answer" question. It can be used, for example, to test for factual knowledge, ability to solve problems or judgment in meeting situations found at work.

A multiple-choice question is normally one of three types—

- It can begin with an incomplete statement followed by several possible endings. You are to find the one ending which *best* completes the statement, although some of the others may not be entirely wrong.
- It can also be a complete statement in the form of a question which is answered by choosing one of the statements listed.

- It can be in the form of a problem – again you select the best answer.

Here is an example of a multiple-choice question with a discussion which should give you some clues as to the method for choosing the right answer:

When an employee has a complaint about his assignment, the action which will *best* help him overcome his difficulty is to

A. discuss his difficulty with his coworkers
B. take the problem to the head of the organization
C. take the problem to the person who gave him the assignment
D. say nothing to anyone about his complaint

In answering this question, you should study each of the choices to find which is best. Consider choice "A" – Certainly an employee may discuss his complaint with fellow employees, but no change or improvement can result, and the complaint remains unresolved. Choice "B" is a poor choice since the head of the organization probably does not know what assignment you have been given, and taking your problem to him is known as "going over the head" of the supervisor. The supervisor, or person who made the assignment, is the person who can clarify it or correct any injustice. Choice "C" is, therefore, correct. To say nothing, as in choice "D," is unwise. Supervisors have and interest in knowing the problems employees are facing, and the employee is seeking a solution to his problem.

2) True/False Questions

The "true/false" or "right/wrong" form of question is sometimes used. Here a complete statement is given. Your job is to decide whether the statement is right or wrong.

SAMPLE: A roaming cell-phone call to a nearby city costs less than a non-roaming call to a distant city.

This statement is wrong, or false, since roaming calls are more expensive.

This is not a complete list of all possible question forms, although most of the others are variations of these common types. You will always get complete directions for answering questions. Be sure you understand *how* to mark your answers – ask questions until you do.

V. RECORDING YOUR ANSWERS

Computer terminals are used more and more today for many different kinds of exams.

For an examination with very few applicants, you may be told to record your answers in the test booklet itself. Separate answer sheets are much more common. If this separate answer sheet is to be scored by machine – and this is often the case – it is highly important that you mark your answers correctly in order to get credit.

An electronic scoring machine is often used in civil service offices because of the speed with which papers can be scored. Machine-scored answer sheets must be marked with a pencil, which will be given to you. This pencil has a high graphite content which responds to the electronic scoring machine. As a matter of fact, stray dots may register as answers, so do not let your pencil rest on the answer sheet while you are pondering the correct answer. Also, if your pencil lead breaks or is otherwise defective, ask for another.

Since the answer sheet will be dropped in a slot in the scoring machine, be careful not to bend the corners or get the paper crumpled.

The answer sheet normally has five vertical columns of numbers, with 30 numbers to a column. These numbers correspond to the question numbers in your test booklet. After each number, going across the page are four or five pairs of dotted lines. These short dotted lines have small letters or numbers above them. The first two pairs may also have a "T" or "F" above the letters. This indicates that the first two pairs only are to be used if the questions are of the true-false type. If the questions are multiple choice, disregard the "T" and "F" and pay attention only to the small letters or numbers.

Answer your questions in the manner of the sample that follows:

32. The largest city in the United States is
    A. Washington, D.C.
    B. New York City
    C. Chicago
    D. Detroit
    E. San Francisco

1) Choose the answer you think is best. (New York City is the largest, so "B" is correct.)
2) Find the row of dotted lines numbered the same as the question you are answering. (Find row number 32)
3) Find the pair of dotted lines corresponding to the answer. (Find the pair of lines under the mark "B.")
4) Make a solid black mark between the dotted lines.

VI. BEFORE THE TEST

Common sense will help you find procedures to follow to get ready for an examination. Too many of us, however, overlook these sensible measures. Indeed, nervousness and fatigue have been found to be the most serious reasons why applicants fail to do their best on civil service tests. Here is a list of reminders:

- Begin your preparation early – Don't wait until the last minute to go scurrying around for books and materials or to find out what the position is all about.
- Prepare continuously – An hour a night for a week is better than an all-night cram session. This has been definitely established. What is more, a night a week for a month will return better dividends than crowding your study into a shorter period of time.
- Locate the place of the exam – You have been sent a notice telling you when and where to report for the examination. If the location is in a different town or otherwise unfamiliar to you, it would be well to inquire the best route and learn something about the building.
- Relax the night before the test – Allow your mind to rest. Do not study at all that night. Plan some mild recreation or diversion; then go to bed early and get a good night's sleep.
- Get up early enough to make a leisurely trip to the place for the test – This way unforeseen events, traffic snarls, unfamiliar buildings, etc. will not upset you.
- Dress comfortably – A written test is not a fashion show. You will be known by number and not by name, so wear something comfortable.

- Leave excess paraphernalia at home – Shopping bags and odd bundles will get in your way. You need bring only the items mentioned in the official notice you received; usually everything you need is provided. Do not bring reference books to the exam. They will only confuse those last minutes and be taken away from you when in the test room.
- Arrive somewhat ahead of time – If because of transportation schedules you must get there very early, bring a newspaper or magazine to take your mind off yourself while waiting.
- Locate the examination room – When you have found the proper room, you will be directed to the seat or part of the room where you will sit. Sometimes you are given a sheet of instructions to read while you are waiting. Do not fill out any forms until you are told to do so; just read them and be prepared.
- Relax and prepare to listen to the instructions
- If you have any physical problem that may keep you from doing your best, be sure to tell the test administrator. If you are sick or in poor health, you really cannot do your best on the exam. You can come back and take the test some other time.

VII. AT THE TEST

The day of the test is here and you have the test booklet in your hand. The temptation to get going is very strong. Caution! There is more to success than knowing the right answers. You must know how to identify your papers and understand variations in the type of short-answer question used in this particular examination. Follow these suggestions for maximum results from your efforts:

1) Cooperate with the monitor

The test administrator has a duty to create a situation in which you can be as much at ease as possible. He will give instructions, tell you when to begin, check to see that you are marking your answer sheet correctly, and so on. He is not there to guard you, although he will see that your competitors do not take unfair advantage. He wants to help you do your best.

2) Listen to all instructions

Don't jump the gun! Wait until you understand all directions. In most civil service tests you get more time than you need to answer the questions. So don't be in a hurry. Read each word of instructions until you clearly understand the meaning. Study the examples, listen to all announcements and follow directions. Ask questions if you do not understand what to do.

3) Identify your papers

Civil service exams are usually identified by number only. You will be assigned a number; you must not put your name on your test papers. Be sure to copy your number correctly. Since more than one exam may be given, copy your exact examination title.

4) Plan your time

Unless you are told that a test is a "speed" or "rate of work" test, speed itself is usually not important. Time enough to answer all the questions will be provided, but this does not mean that you have all day. An overall time limit has been set. Divide the total time (in minutes) by the number of questions to determine the approximate time you have for each question.

5) Do not linger over difficult questions

If you come across a difficult question, mark it with a paper clip (useful to have along) and come back to it when you have been through the booklet. One caution if you do this – be sure to skip a number on your answer sheet as well. Check often to be sure that you have not lost your place and that you are marking in the row numbered the same as the question you are answering.

6) Read the questions

Be sure you know what the question asks! Many capable people are unsuccessful because they failed to *read* the questions correctly.

7) Answer all questions

Unless you have been instructed that a penalty will be deducted for incorrect answers, it is better to guess than to omit a question.

8) Speed tests

It is often better NOT to guess on speed tests. It has been found that on timed tests people are tempted to spend the last few seconds before time is called in marking answers at random – without even reading them – in the hope of picking up a few extra points. To discourage this practice, the instructions may warn you that your score will be "corrected" for guessing. That is, a penalty will be applied. The incorrect answers will be deducted from the correct ones, or some other penalty formula will be used.

9) Review your answers

If you finish before time is called, go back to the questions you guessed or omitted to give them further thought. Review other answers if you have time.

10) Return your test materials

If you are ready to leave before others have finished or time is called, take ALL your materials to the monitor and leave quietly. Never take any test material with you. The monitor can discover whose papers are not complete, and taking a test booklet may be grounds for disqualification.

VIII. EXAMINATION TECHNIQUES

1) Read the general instructions carefully. These are usually printed on the first page of the exam booklet. As a rule, these instructions refer to the timing of the examination; the fact that you should not start work until the signal and must stop work at a signal, etc. If there are any *special* instructions, such as a choice of questions to be answered, make sure that you note this instruction carefully.

2) When you are ready to start work on the examination, that is as soon as the signal has been given, read the instructions to each question booklet, underline any key words or phrases, such as *least*, *best*, *outline*, *describe* and the like. In this way you will tend to answer as requested rather than discover on reviewing your paper that you *listed without describing*, that you selected the *worst* choice rather than the *best* choice, etc.

3) If the examination is of the objective or multiple-choice type – that is, each question will also give a series of possible answers: A, B, C or D, and you are called upon to select the best answer and write the letter next to that answer on your answer paper – it is advisable to start answering each question in turn. There may be anywhere from 50 to 100 such questions in the three or four hours allotted and you can see how much time would be taken if you read through all the questions before beginning to answer any. Furthermore, if you come across a question or group of questions which you know would be difficult to answer, it would undoubtedly affect your handling of all the other questions.

4) If the examination is of the essay type and contains but a few questions, it is a moot point as to whether you should read all the questions before starting to answer any one. Of course, if you are given a choice – say five out of seven and the like – then it is essential to read all the questions so you can eliminate the two that are most difficult. If, however, you are asked to answer all the questions, there may be danger in trying to answer the easiest one first because you may find that you will spend too much time on it. The best technique is to answer the first question, then proceed to the second, etc.

5) Time your answers. Before the exam begins, write down the time it started, then add the time allowed for the examination and write down the time it must be completed, then divide the time available somewhat as follows:
   - If 3-1/2 hours are allowed, that would be 210 minutes. If you have 80 objective-type questions, that would be an average of 2-1/2 minutes per question. Allow yourself no more than 2 minutes per question, or a total of 160 minutes, which will permit about 50 minutes to review.
   - If for the time allotment of 210 minutes there are 7 essay questions to answer, that would average about 30 minutes a question. Give yourself only 25 minutes per question so that you have about 35 minutes to review.

6) The most important instruction is to *read each question* and make sure you know what is wanted. The second most important instruction is to *time yourself properly* so that you answer every question. The third most important instruction is to *answer every question*. Guess if you have to but include something for each question. Remember that you will receive no credit for a blank and will probably receive some credit if you write something in answer to an essay question. If you guess a letter – say "B" for a multiple-choice question – you may have guessed right. If you leave a blank as an answer to a multiple-choice question, the examiners may respect your feelings but it will not add a point to your score. Some exams may penalize you for wrong answers, so in such cases *only*, you may not want to guess unless you have some basis for your answer.

7) Suggestions
   a. Objective-type questions
      1. Examine the question booklet for proper sequence of pages and questions
      2. Read all instructions carefully
      3. Skip any question which seems too difficult; return to it after all other questions have been answered
      4. Apportion your time properly; do not spend too much time on any single question or group of questions

5. Note and underline key words – *all, most, fewest, least, best, worst, same, opposite,* etc.
6. Pay particular attention to negatives
7. Note unusual option, e.g., unduly long, short, complex, different or similar in content to the body of the question
8. Observe the use of "hedging" words – *probably, may, most likely,* etc.
9. Make sure that your answer is put next to the same number as the question
10. Do not second-guess unless you have good reason to believe the second answer is definitely more correct
11. Cross out original answer if you decide another answer is more accurate; do not erase until you are ready to hand your paper in
12. Answer all questions; guess unless instructed otherwise
13. Leave time for review

b. Essay questions
1. Read each question carefully
2. Determine exactly what is wanted. Underline key words or phrases.
3. Decide on outline or paragraph answer
4. Include many different points and elements unless asked to develop any one or two points or elements
5. Show impartiality by giving pros and cons unless directed to select one side only
6. Make and write down any assumptions you find necessary to answer the questions
7. Watch your English, grammar, punctuation and choice of words
8. Time your answers; don't crowd material

8) Answering the essay question

Most essay questions can be answered by framing the specific response around several key words or ideas. Here are a few such key words or ideas:

M's: manpower, materials, methods, money, management
P's: purpose, program, policy, plan, procedure, practice, problems, pitfalls, personnel, public relations

a. Six basic steps in handling problems:
1. Preliminary plan and background development
2. Collect information, data and facts
3. Analyze and interpret information, data and facts
4. Analyze and develop solutions as well as make recommendations
5. Prepare report and sell recommendations
6. Install recommendations and follow up effectiveness

b. Pitfalls to avoid
1. *Taking things for granted* – A statement of the situation does not necessarily imply that each of the elements is necessarily true; for example, a complaint may be invalid and biased so that all that can be taken for granted is that a complaint has been registered

2. *Considering only one side of a situation* – Wherever possible, indicate several alternatives and then point out the reasons you selected the best one
3. *Failing to indicate follow up* – Whenever your answer indicates action on your part, make certain that you will take proper follow-up action to see how successful your recommendations, procedures or actions turn out to be
4. *Taking too long in answering any single question* – Remember to time your answers properly

IX. AFTER THE TEST

Scoring procedures differ in detail among civil service jurisdictions although the general principles are the same. Whether the papers are hand-scored or graded by machine we have described, they are nearly always graded by number. That is, the person who marks the paper knows only the number – never the name – of the applicant. Not until all the papers have been graded will they be matched with names. If other tests, such as training and experience or oral interview ratings have been given, scores will be combined. Different parts of the examination usually have different weights. For example, the written test might count 60 percent of the final grade, and a rating of training and experience 40 percent. In many jurisdictions, veterans will have a certain number of points added to their grades.

After the final grade has been determined, the names are placed in grade order and an eligible list is established. There are various methods for resolving ties between those who get the same final grade – probably the most common is to place first the name of the person whose application was received first. Job offers are made from the eligible list in the order the names appear on it. You will be notified of your grade and your rank as soon as all these computations have been made. This will be done as rapidly as possible.

People who are found to meet the requirements in the announcement are called "eligibles." Their names are put on a list of eligible candidates. An eligible's chances of getting a job depend on how high he stands on this list and how fast agencies are filling jobs from the list.

When a job is to be filled from a list of eligibles, the agency asks for the names of people on the list of eligibles for that job. When the civil service commission receives this request, it sends to the agency the names of the three people highest on this list. Or, if the job to be filled has specialized requirements, the office sends the agency the names of the top three persons who meet these requirements from the general list.

The appointing officer makes a choice from among the three people whose names were sent to him. If the selected person accepts the appointment, the names of the others are put back on the list to be considered for future openings.

That is the rule in hiring from all kinds of eligible lists, whether they are for typist, carpenter, chemist, or something else. For every vacancy, the appointing officer has his choice of any one of the top three eligibles on the list. This explains why the person whose name is on top of the list sometimes does not get an appointment when some of the persons lower on the list do. If the appointing officer chooses the second or third eligible, the No. 1 eligible does not get a job at once, but stays on the list until he is appointed or the list is terminated.

X. HOW TO PASS THE INTERVIEW TEST

The examination for which you applied requires an oral interview test. You have already taken the written test and you are now being called for the interview test – the final part of the formal examination.

You may think that it is not possible to prepare for an interview test and that there are no procedures to follow during an interview. Our purpose is to point out some things you can do in advance that will help you and some good rules to follow and pitfalls to avoid while you are being interviewed.

What is an interview supposed to test?

The written examination is designed to test the technical knowledge and competence of the candidate; the oral is designed to evaluate intangible qualities, not readily measured otherwise, and to establish a list showing the relative fitness of each candidate – as measured against his competitors – for the position sought. Scoring is not on the basis of "right" and "wrong," but on a sliding scale of values ranging from "not passable" to "outstanding." As a matter of fact, it is possible to achieve a relatively low score without a single "incorrect" answer because of evident weakness in the qualities being measured.

Occasionally, an examination may consist entirely of an oral test – either an individual or a group oral. In such cases, information is sought concerning the technical knowledges and abilities of the candidate, since there has been no written examination for this purpose. More commonly, however, an oral test is used to supplement a written examination.

Who conducts interviews?

The composition of oral boards varies among different jurisdictions. In nearly all, a representative of the personnel department serves as chairman. One of the members of the board may be a representative of the department in which the candidate would work. In some cases, "outside experts" are used, and, frequently, a businessman or some other representative of the general public is asked to serve. Labor and management or other special groups may be represented. The aim is to secure the services of experts in the appropriate field.

However the board is composed, it is a good idea (and not at all improper or unethical) to ascertain in advance of the interview who the members are and what groups they represent. When you are introduced to them, you will have some idea of their backgrounds and interests, and at least you will not stutter and stammer over their names.

What should be done before the interview?

While knowledge about the board members is useful and takes some of the surprise element out of the interview, there is other preparation which is more substantive. It *is* possible to prepare for an oral interview – in several ways:

1) Keep a copy of your application and review it carefully before the interview

This may be the only document before the oral board, and the starting point of the interview. Know what education and experience you have listed there, and the sequence and dates of all of it. Sometimes the board will ask you to review the highlights of your experience for them; you should not have to hem and haw doing it.

2) Study the class specification and the examination announcement

Usually, the oral board has one or both of these to guide them. The qualities, characteristics or knowledges required by the position sought are stated in these documents. They offer valuable clues as to the nature of the oral interview. For example, if the job involves supervisory responsibilities, the announcement will usually indicate that knowledge of modern supervisory methods and the qualifications of the candidate as a supervisor will be tested. If so, you can expect such questions, frequently in the form of a hypothetical situation which you are expected to solve. NEVER go into an oral without knowledge of the duties and responsibilities of the job you seek.

3) Think through each qualification required

Try to visualize the kind of questions you would ask if you were a board member. How well could you answer them? Try especially to appraise your own knowledge and background in each area, *measured against the job sought*, and identify any areas in which you are weak. Be critical and realistic – do not flatter yourself.

4) Do some general reading in areas in which you feel you may be weak

For example, if the job involves supervision and your past experience has NOT, some general reading in supervisory methods and practices, particularly in the field of human relations, might be useful. Do NOT study agency procedures or detailed manuals. The oral board will be testing your understanding and capacity, not your memory.

5) Get a good night's sleep and watch your general health and mental attitude

You will want a clear head at the interview. Take care of a cold or any other minor ailment, and of course, no hangovers.

What should be done on the day of the interview?

Now comes the day of the interview itself. Give yourself plenty of time to get there. Plan to arrive somewhat ahead of the scheduled time, particularly if your appointment is in the fore part of the day. If a previous candidate fails to appear, the board might be ready for you a bit early. By early afternoon an oral board is almost invariably behind schedule if there are many candidates, and you may have to wait. Take along a book or magazine to read, or your application to review, but leave any extraneous material in the waiting room when you go in for your interview. In any event, relax and compose yourself.

The matter of dress is important. The board is forming impressions about you – from your experience, your manners, your attitude, and your appearance. Give your personal appearance careful attention. Dress your best, but not your flashiest. Choose conservative, appropriate clothing, and be sure it is immaculate. This is a business interview, and your appearance should indicate that you regard it as such. Besides, being well groomed and properly dressed will help boost your confidence.

Sooner or later, someone will call your name and escort you into the interview room. *This is it.* From here on you are on your own. It is too late for any more preparation. But remember, you asked for this opportunity to prove your fitness, and you are here because your request was granted.

What happens when you go in?

The usual sequence of events will be as follows: The clerk (who is often the board stenographer) will introduce you to the chairman of the oral board, who will introduce you to the other members of the board. Acknowledge the introductions before you sit down. Do not be surprised if you find a microphone facing you or a stenotypist sitting by. Oral interviews are usually recorded in the event of an appeal or other review.

Usually the chairman of the board will open the interview by reviewing the highlights of your education and work experience from your application – primarily for the benefit of the other members of the board, as well as to get the material into the record. Do not interrupt or comment unless there is an error or significant misinterpretation; if that is the case, do not hesitate. But do not quibble about insignificant matters. Also, he will usually ask you some question about your education, experience or your present job – partly to get you to start talking and to establish the interviewing "rapport." He may start the actual questioning, or turn it over to one of the other members. Frequently, each member undertakes the questioning on a particular area, one in which he is perhaps most competent, so you can expect each member to participate in the examination. Because time is limited, you may also expect some rather abrupt switches in the direction the questioning takes, so do not be upset by it. Normally, a board member will not pursue a single line of questioning unless he discovers a particular strength or weakness.

After each member has participated, the chairman will usually ask whether any member has any further questions, then will ask you if you have anything you wish to add. Unless you are expecting this question, it may floor you. Worse, it may start you off on an extended, extemporaneous speech. The board is not usually seeking more information. The question is principally to offer you a last opportunity to present further qualifications or to indicate that you have nothing to add. So, if you feel that a significant qualification or characteristic has been overlooked, it is proper to point it out in a sentence or so. Do not compliment the board on the thoroughness of their examination – they have been sketchy, and you know it. If you wish, merely say, "No thank you, I have nothing further to add." This is a point where you can "talk yourself out" of a good impression or fail to present an important bit of information. Remember, *you close the interview yourself.*

The chairman will then say, "That is all, Mr. _______, thank you." Do not be startled; the interview is over, and quicker than you think. Thank him, gather your belongings and take your leave. Save your sigh of relief for the other side of the door.

How to put your best foot forward

Throughout this entire process, you may feel that the board individually and collectively is trying to pierce your defenses, seek out your hidden weaknesses and embarrass and confuse you. Actually, this is not true. They are obliged to make an appraisal of your qualifications for the job you are seeking, and they want to see you in your best light. Remember, they must interview all candidates and a non-cooperative candidate may become a failure in spite of their best efforts to bring out his qualifications. Here are 15 suggestions that will help you:

1) Be natural – Keep your attitude confident, not cocky

If you are not confident that you can do the job, do not expect the board to be. Do not apologize for your weaknesses, try to bring out your strong points. The board is interested in a positive, not negative, presentation. Cockiness will antagonize any board member and make him wonder if you are covering up a weakness by a false show of strength.

2) Get comfortable, but don't lounge or sprawl

Sit erectly but not stiffly. A careless posture may lead the board to conclude that you are careless in other things, or at least that you are not impressed by the importance of the occasion. Either conclusion is natural, even if incorrect. Do not fuss with your clothing, a pencil or an ashtray. Your hands may occasionally be useful to emphasize a point; do not let them become a point of distraction.

3) Do not wisecrack or make small talk

This is a serious situation, and your attitude should show that you consider it as such. Further, the time of the board is limited – they do not want to waste it, and neither should you.

4) Do not exaggerate your experience or abilities

In the first place, from information in the application or other interviews and sources, the board may know more about you than you think. Secondly, you probably will not get away with it. An experienced board is rather adept at spotting such a situation, so do not take the chance.

5) If you know a board member, do not make a point of it, yet do not hide it

Certainly you are not fooling him, and probably not the other members of the board. Do not try to take advantage of your acquaintanceship – it will probably do you little good.

6) Do not dominate the interview

Let the board do that. They will give you the clues – do not assume that you have to do all the talking. Realize that the board has a number of questions to ask you, and do not try to take up all the interview time by showing off your extensive knowledge of the answer to the first one.

7) Be attentive

You only have 20 minutes or so, and you should keep your attention at its sharpest throughout. When a member is addressing a problem or question to you, give him your undivided attention. Address your reply principally to him, but do not exclude the other board members.

8) Do not interrupt

A board member may be stating a problem for you to analyze. He will ask you a question when the time comes. Let him state the problem, and wait for the question.

9) Make sure you understand the question

Do not try to answer until you are sure what the question is. If it is not clear, restate it in your own words or ask the board member to clarify it for you. However, do not haggle about minor elements.

10) Reply promptly but not hastily

A common entry on oral board rating sheets is "candidate responded readily," or "candidate hesitated in replies." Respond as promptly and quickly as you can, but do not jump to a hasty, ill-considered answer.

11) Do not be peremptory in your answers

A brief answer is proper – but do not fire your answer back. That is a losing game from your point of view. The board member can probably ask questions much faster than you can answer them.

12) Do not try to create the answer you think the board member wants

He is interested in what kind of mind you have and how it works – not in playing games. Furthermore, he can usually spot this practice and will actually grade you down on it.

13) Do not switch sides in your reply merely to agree with a board member

Frequently, a member will take a contrary position merely to draw you out and to see if you are willing and able to defend your point of view. Do not start a debate, yet do not surrender a good position. If a position is worth taking, it is worth defending.

14) Do not be afraid to admit an error in judgment if you are shown to be wrong

The board knows that you are forced to reply without any opportunity for careful consideration. Your answer may be demonstrably wrong. If so, admit it and get on with the interview.

15) Do not dwell at length on your present job

The opening question may relate to your present assignment. Answer the question but do not go into an extended discussion. You are being examined for a *new* job, not your present one. As a matter of fact, try to phrase ALL your answers in terms of the job for which you are being examined.

Basis of Rating

Probably you will forget most of these "do's" and "don'ts" when you walk into the oral interview room. Even remembering them all will not ensure you a passing grade. Perhaps you did not have the qualifications in the first place. But remembering them will help you to put your best foot forward, without treading on the toes of the board members.

Rumor and popular opinion to the contrary notwithstanding, an oral board wants you to make the best appearance possible. They know you are under pressure – but they also want to see how you respond to it as a guide to what your reaction would be under the pressures of the job you seek. They will be influenced by the degree of poise you display, the personal traits you show and the manner in which you respond.

ABOUT THIS BOOK

This book contains tests divided into Examination Sections. Go through each test, answering every question in the margin. We have also attached a sample answer sheet at the back of the book that can be removed and used. At the end of each test look at the answer key and check your answers. On the ones you got wrong, look at the right answer choice and learn. Do not fill in the answers first. Do not memorize the questions and answers, but understand the answer and principles involved. On your test, the questions will likely be different from the samples. Questions are changed and new ones added. If you understand these past questions you should have success with any changes that arise. Tests may consist of several types of questions. We have additional books on each subject should more study be advisable or necessary for you. Finally, the more you study, the better prepared you will be. This book is intended to be the last thing you study before you walk into the examination room. Prior study of relevant texts is also recommended. NLC publishes some of these in our Fundamental Series. Knowledge and good sense are important factors in passing your exam. Good luck also helps. So now study this Passbook, absorb the material contained within and take that knowledge into the examination. Then do your best to pass that exam.

EXAMINATION SECTION

EXAMINATION SECTION
TEST 1

DIRECTIONS: Each question or incomplete statement is followed by several suggested answers or completions. Select the one that BEST answers the question or completes the statement. *PRINT THE LETTER OF THE CORRECT ANSWER IN THE SPACE AT THE RIGHT.*

1. A stenographer can BEST deal with the situation which arises when her pencil breaks during dictation by 1.____

   A. asking the person dictating to lend her one
   B. going back to her desk to secure another one
   C. being equipped at every dictation with several pencils
   D. making a call to the supply room for some pencils

2. Accuracy is of greater importance than speed in filing CHIEFLY because 2.____

   A. city offices have a tremendous amount of filing to do
   B. fast workers are usually inferior workers
   C. there is considerable difficulty in locating materials which have been filed incorrectly
   D. there are many varieties of filing systems which may be used

3. Many persons dictate so rapidly that they pay little attention to matters of punctuation and English, but they expect their stenographers to correct errors. This statement implies MOST clearly that stenographers should be 3.____

   A. able to write acceptable original reports when required
   B. good citizens as well as good stenographers
   C. efficient clerks as well as good stenographers
   D. efficient in language usage

4. A typed letter should resemble a picture properly framed. This statement MOST emphasizes 4.____

   A. accuracy
   B. speed
   C. convenience
   D. neatness

5. Of the following, the CHIEF advantage of the use of a mechanical check is that it 5.____

   A. guards against tearing in handling the check
   B. decreases the possibility of alteration in the amount of the check
   C. tends to prevent the mislaying and loss of checks
   D. facilitates keeping checks in proper order for mailing

6. Of the following, the CHIEF advantage of the use of a dictating machine is that the 6.____

   A. stenographer must be able to take rapid dictation
   B. person dictating tends to make few errors
   C. dictator may be dictating letters while the stenographer is busy at some other task
   D. usual noise in an office is lessened

7. The CHIEF value of indicating enclosures beneath the identification marks on the lower left side of a letter is that it 7.____

   A. acts as a check upon the contents before mailing and upon receiving a letter
   B. helps determine the weight for mailing
   C. is useful in checking the accuracy of typed matter
   D. requires an efficient mailing clerk

8. The one of the following which is NOT an advantage of the window envelope is that it 8.____

   A. saves time since the inside address serves also as an outside address
   B. gives protection to the address from wear and tear of the mails
   C. lessens the possibility of mistakes since the address is written only once
   D. tends to be much easier to seal than the plain envelope

9. A question as to proper syllabication of a word at the end of a line may BEST be settled by consulting 9.____

   A. the person who dictated the letter
   B. a shorthand manual
   C. a dictionary
   D. a file of letters

10. Mailing a letter which contains many erasures is UNDESIRABLE chiefly because 10.____

    A. paper should not be wasted
    B. some stenographers are able to carry on some of the correspondence in an office without consulting their superiors
    C. correspondence should be neat
    D. erasures indicate that the dictator was not certain of what he intended to say in the letter

11. Systematizing for efficiency means MOST NEARLY 11.____

    A. performing an assignment despite all interruptions
    B. leaving difficult assignments until the next day
    C. having a definite time schedule for certain daily duties
    D. trying to do as few letters a day as possible

12. The CHIEF value of good paragraphing is that 12.____

    A. it is an aid to the stenographer because it shortens letters
    B. the stenographer who uses it will make few errors in her letters
    C. it saves time for the typist
    D. it aids the reader in understanding the whole letter

13. If postage stamps or seals are so placed on a parcel post package that they seal it against inspection, the package must be sent as ______ mail. 13.____

    A. first class
    B. second class
    C. third class
    D. special delivery

14. The emergency relief bureau was especially designed to aid 14.____

A. the needy unemployed
B. homeless men
C. homeowners unable to keep up with mortgage payments
D. needy persons from other parts of the country who had come in search of a job

15. In many cities, immense expense is incurred in straightening streets, removing buildings, and cutting new streets to relieve traffic congestion, filling in and beautifying river and lake fronts, and building parks and playgrounds in places convenient for the people. The necessity of this type of expense is BEST avoided by 15.____

A. planning
B. reducing expenditures
C. a central bureau for purchasing and spending
D. appropriate changes in the tax rate

16. The city charter operates for the city in somewhat the SAME fashion as 16.____

A. the United States Supreme Court functions with regard to federal legislation
B. the United States Constitution operates for the entire country
C. the Governor functions for the state
D. P.R. operates in the city

17. The municipal employee should be interested in the activities of the United States Supreme Court PRIMARILY because 17.____

A. its decisions provide certain kinds of important general rules
B. the Supreme Court consists of nine persons appointed by the President
C. the American Constitution is the finest document which man has ever produced
D. the President's plan for reorganization of the court may be revived

18. Of the following, it is most frequently argued that labor problems are of concern to the municipal employee PRIMARILY because 18.____

A. the problems of labor are the same as the problems of municipal government
B. newspapers carry considerable information about labor problems
C. the municipal employee is a wage or salary earner
D. a municipal government is of the people, for the people, and by the people

19. Warfare in any part of the world should be of interest to the municipal employee PRIMARILY as a result of the fact that 19.____

A. strict American neutrality is secured by not permitting the sale of munitions to any country at war
B. war has not been declared though warfare is raging
C. the United States frequently participates in the meetings of the United Nations
D. facilities for transportation and communication have produced a *smaller* world

20. The city regulates certain aspects of housing CHIEFLY because 20.____

A. the city is the largest municipality in the country
B. zoning is the concern of all residents of the city

C. housing affects health
D. the state Constitution makes regulation optional

21. In general, it is probably true that the functions which the city administers are those 21.____

A. most necessary to the preservation of the well-being of its residents
B. of little or no interest to private business
C. forbidden to the state
D. not capable of being financed by private business

22. The one of the following which is NOT a regular city department is 22.____

A. Public Welfare
B. Libraries
C. Purchase
D. Sanitation

23. The present outlook on social work has become different ______ that of the past. 23.____

A. by
B. to
C. with
D. from

KEY (CORRECT ANSWERS)

1. C
2. C
3. D
4. D
5. B

6. C
7. A
8. D
9. C
10. C

11. C
12. D
13. A
14. A
15. A

16. B
17. A
18. C
19. D
20. C

21. A
22. B
23. D

TEST 2

DIRECTIONS: Each question or incomplete statement is followed by several suggested answers or completions. Select the one that BEST answers the question or completes the statement. *PRINT THE LETTER OF THE CORRECT ANSWER IN THE SPACE AT THE RIGHT.*

1. *Re* is MOST frequently read as the abbreviation for 1.____

   A. in regard to B. real estate
   C. receipt D. return enclosure

2. *Prox.* is MOST frequently read as the abbreviation for 2.____

   A. approximate balance B. last month
   C. next month D. by proxy

3. In alphabetical filing, abbreviations such as *Wm.* or *Chas.* are 3.____

   A. disregarded entirely
   B. treated as if spelled out
   C. disregarded except for first letter
   D. placed in parentheses and disregarded

4. Confusion regarding the exact location of certain papers missing from files can probably BEST be avoided by 4.____

   A. using colored tabs
   B. using the Dewey Decimal System
   C. making files available to few persons
   D. consistently using *out* guides

5. On payment of proper fees, special handling is given to ______ mail. 5.____

   A. all B. first class
   C. second class D. fourth class

6. The MAXIMUM weight of packages which can be sent by fourth class mail is ______ pounds. 6.____

   A. 70 B. 50 C. 100 D. 25

7. The CHIEF advantage of a night letter over a telegram is probably 7.____

   A. speed B. economy
   C. brevity D. dependability

8. The regular monthly rate charged for telephone service pays for all 8.____

   A. outgoing calls made during the month
   B. outgoing local calls up to a certain number
   C. calls including a stated number of out-of-town calls
   D. calls except out-of-town calls

9. Property tax is computed on 9.____

   A. actual value B. purchase price
   C. assessed valuation D. amount of first mortgage

10. The abbreviation *N.B.* means 10.____

A. disregard
B. no good
C. does not belong
D. note carefully

11. Of the following, the one which is NOT one of the values of the typewritten signature in a business letter is that the 11.____

A. receiver can read the typewritten signature if the ink signature is not legible
B. typewritten signature leaves a record on carbon copies for a reference regarding signer
C. signer may simply initial above the typewritten signature if he so desires
D. typewritten signature indicates that the contents of the letter have been checked by the sender

12. There is no more convincing mark of a cultured speaker or writer than accuracy of statement. 12.____
This statement stressed the importance of

A. new ideas
B. facts
C. acquiring a pleasing speaking voice
D. poise

13. When a department is called, the voice which answers the telephone is, to the person calling, the department itself. This statement implies MOST clearly that 13.____

A. only one person should answer the telephone in each office
B. a clerk with a pleasing, courteous telephone manner is an asset to an office
C. an efficient clerk will terminate all telephone conversations as quickly as possible
D. making personal telephone calls is looked upon with disfavor in some offices

14. Probably the CHIEF advantage of filling higher vacancies by promotion is that this procedure 14.____

A. stimulates the worker to improve his work and general knowledge and technique
B. provides an easy check on the work of the individual
C. eliminates personnel problems in a department
D. harmonizes the work of one department with that of all other departments

15. Greatest efficiency is reached when filing method and filing clerk are harmoniously adjusted to the needs of an office. 15.____
This statement means MOST NEARLY that

A. the filing method is more important than the clerk in securing the successful handling of valuable papers
B. almost any clerk can do office filing well
C. a good clerk using a good filing system assures good filing
D. every office needs a filing system

KEY (CORRECT ANSWERS)

1. A
2. C
3. B
4. D
5. D
6. A
7. B
8. B
9. C
10. D
11. D
12. B
13. B
14. A
15. C

TEST 3

DIRECTIONS: Each question or incomplete statement is followed by several suggested answers or completions. Select the one that BEST answers the question or completes the statement. *PRINT THE LETTER OF THE CORRECT ANSWER IN THE SPACE AT THE RIGHT.*

1. Your superior, Mr. Hotchkiss, is in conference and has requested that he not be disturbed. 1._____
   The condition under which you would MOST probably disturb the conference is:

   A. A Mr. Smith, whom you have not seen before, says he has important business with Mr. Hotchkiss
   B. Mrs. Hotchkiss telephones, saying there has been a serious accident at home
   C. You do not know how a certain letter should be filed and wish to ask the advice of Mr. Hotchkiss
   D. A fellow clerk wishes to ask Mr. Hotchkiss whether a particular city department handles certain matters

2. Your superior directs you to find certain papers. You know the purpose for which the papers are to be used. In the course of your search for the papers, you come across certain material which would be very useful for the purpose to be served by the papers. 2._____
   You should

   A. bring the papers to your superior and ask whether he wants the other materials
   B. go to your superior immediately and ask whether he wishes both the materials and the papers or only one of the two
   C. bring to your superior the other materials together with the papers you were directed to find
   D. bring only the other materials to your superior and point out the manner in which these materials are of greater value than the papers

3. If a fellow employee asks you a question to which you do not know the answer, you should say, 3._____

   A. I don't know. What's the difference?
   B. The answer to that question forms no part of my duties here.
   C. My dear sir, the thing for you to do is to look the matter up yourself because it is your responsibility, not mine.
   D. I'm sorry. I don't know.

4. In general, it is probably true that MOST people are 4._____

   A. so self-seeking that they pay no attention to the wants, needs, or behavior of others
   B. so changeable that one never knows what his fellow employee is likely to do next
   C. not worth the trouble to bother about
   D. quite ready to help others

5. Of the following, the one which is NOT a reason for avoiding clerical errors is that 5._____

   A. time is lost
   B. money is wasted

C. many clerks are very intelligent
D. serious consequences may follow

6. Of the following, the MAIN reason for keeping a careful record of incoming mail is that 6.____

A. some people are less industrious than others
B. this record helps to speed up outgoing mail
C. this record is a kind of legal evidence
D. this information may be useful in answering questions which may arise

7. Of the following, the MAIN reason for using a calculating machine is that 7.____

A. a lesser knowledge of arithmetic is needed
B. a more attractive product is obtained
C. greater speed and accuracy are obtained
D. it is not difficult to learn how to operate a calculating machine

8. Of the following, the MAIN reason for being polite over the telephone is that 8.____

A. persons who are speaking over the telephone cannot see each other
B. politeness makes for pleasant business relationships
C. it is not at all difficult or costly to be courteous
D. one's voice is of great importance because voice reflects mood

9. Because telephone directories contain printed pages, they are called books. 9.____
This statement assumes MOST NEARLY that

A. some books do not contain printed pages
B. not all telephone directories are books which contain printed pages
C. material which contains printed pages is called a book
D. all books which contain printed pages are called telephone directories

10. Mr. Cross must be using a budget because he has been able to reduce his unnecessary expenses. 10.____
On the basis of only the material included in this statement, it may MOST accurately be said that this statement assumes that

A. all people who use budgets lower certain types of expenses
B. some people who do not use budgets reduce unnecessary expenses
C. some people who use budgets do not reduce unnecessary expenses
D. all types of expenses are reduced by the use of a budget

11. Of the following, the MAIN purpose of tabulating a set of figures is that 11.____

A. interpretation is facilitated
B. computational accuracy is assured
C. pictorial representations lend themselves to easy evaluation
D. any set of figures must be based upon prior arithmetical calculations

12. Of the following, the LEAST important characteristic of a good tabular presentation of data is that 12.____

A. decimals are rounded off to the nearest whole number
B. the title appears at the top

C. entries are correct
D. the title is brief

13. To print tabular material is always much more expensive than to print straight text. It follows MOST NEARLY that 13.____

A. the more columns and subdivisions there are in a table, the more expensive is the printing
B. the omission of the number and title from a table greatly reduces the expense of printing
C. it is always desirable to substitute text for tabular material
D. a graphic presentation should almost always be substituted for a table in order to save money

14. The circumstances under which a person-to-person telephone call should be made occur when the person calling 14.____

A. wishes to make the least expensive type of telephone call
B. is certain that the person to be called is at his desk waiting for the call
C. believes that the person to be called is not likely to be present to receive the call
D. is seeking information which is probably known by all the members of an office, rather than only a single person

15. A check which customarily states on its face the purpose for which the money is paid is MOST probably termed a ______ check. 15.____

A. certified
B. cashier's
C. voucher
D. personal

KEY (CORRECT ANSWERS)

1. B
2. C
3. D
4. D
5. C
6. D
7. C
8. B
9. C
10. A
11. A
12. A
13. A
14. C
15. C

TEST 4

DIRECTIONS: Each question or incomplete statement is followed by several suggested answers or completions. Select the one that BEST answers the question or completes the statement. *PRINT THE LETTER OF THE CORRECT ANSWER IN THE SPACE AT THE RIGHT.*

1. The BEST arrangement of folder tabs for easy location of material in the files is 1.____

   A. staggered from left to right
   B. zigzagged in alternate positions
   C. staggered from right to left
   D. placed in one center position, one tab directly behind the other

2. Generally speaking (without regard to special localities where there might be a preponderance of like names), the letter in the alphabet requiring the MOST captions for guides in a breakdown or division of the alphabet is the letter 2.____

   A. B B. C C. M D. S

3. In filing terminology, coding means 3.____

   A. making a preliminary arrangement of names according to caption before bringing them together in final order of arrangement
   B. reading correspondence and determining the proper caption under which it is to be filed
   C. marking a card or paper with symbols or other means of identification to indicate where it is to be placed in the files according to a predetermined plan
   D. placing a card or paper in the files showing where correspondence may be located under another name or title

4. A duplex-number system of filing is a(n) 4.____

   A. decimal system
   B. arrangement of guides and folders with a definite color scheme to aid in filing and locating material
   C. system of filing by which classified subjects are divided and subdivided by number for the purpose of expansion
   D. method of filing names according to sound instead of spelling

Questions 5-7.

DIRECTIONS: Questions 5 through 7 are to be answered SOLELY on the basis of information contained in the following passage.

It is common knowledge that ability to do a particular job and performance on the job do not always go hand in hand. Persons with great potential abilities sometimes fall down on the job because of laziness or lack of interest in the job, while persons with mediocre talents have often achieved excellent results through their industry and their loyalty to the interests of their employers. It is clear, therefore, that in a balanced personnel program, measures of employee ability need to be supplemented by measures of employee performance, for the final test of any employee is his performance on the job.

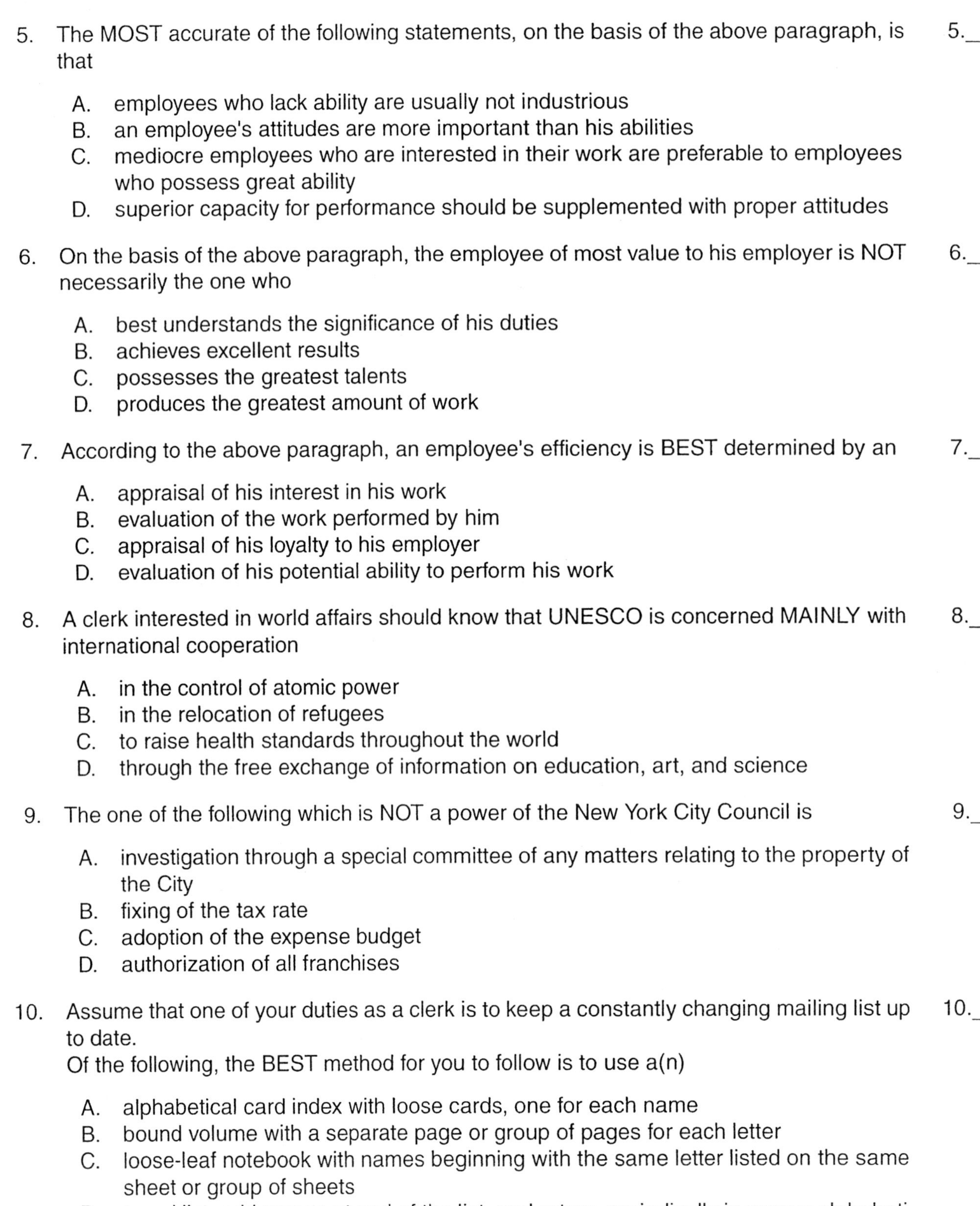

5. The MOST accurate of the following statements, on the basis of the above paragraph, is that 5.___

   A. employees who lack ability are usually not industrious
   B. an employee's attitudes are more important than his abilities
   C. mediocre employees who are interested in their work are preferable to employees who possess great ability
   D. superior capacity for performance should be supplemented with proper attitudes

6. On the basis of the above paragraph, the employee of most value to his employer is NOT necessarily the one who 6.___

   A. best understands the significance of his duties
   B. achieves excellent results
   C. possesses the greatest talents
   D. produces the greatest amount of work

7. According to the above paragraph, an employee's efficiency is BEST determined by an 7.___

   A. appraisal of his interest in his work
   B. evaluation of the work performed by him
   C. appraisal of his loyalty to his employer
   D. evaluation of his potential ability to perform his work

8. A clerk interested in world affairs should know that UNESCO is concerned MAINLY with international cooperation 8.___

   A. in the control of atomic power
   B. in the relocation of refugees
   C. to raise health standards throughout the world
   D. through the free exchange of information on education, art, and science

9. The one of the following which is NOT a power of the New York City Council is 9.___

   A. investigation through a special committee of any matters relating to the property of the City
   B. fixing of the tax rate
   C. adoption of the expense budget
   D. authorization of all franchises

10. Assume that one of your duties as a clerk is to keep a constantly changing mailing list up to date. 10.___
    Of the following, the BEST method for you to follow is to use a(n)

   A. alphabetical card index with loose cards, one for each name
   B. bound volume with a separate page or group of pages for each letter
   C. loose-leaf notebook with names beginning with the same letter listed on the same sheet or group of sheets
   D. typed list, add names at end of the list, and retype periodically in proper alphabetical order

11. In evaluating the effectiveness of a filing system, the one of the following criteria which you should consider MOST important is the 11.____

   A. safety of material in the event of a fire
   B. ease with which material may be located
   C. quantity of papers which can be filed
   D. extent to which material in the filing systems is being used

12. A set of cards numbered from 1 to 300 has been filed in numerical order in such a way that the highest number is at the front of the file and lowest number is at the rear. It is desired that the cards be reversed to run in ascending order. 12.____
The BEST of the following methods that can be used in performing this task is to begin at the

   A. front of the file and remove the cards one at a time, placing each one face up on top of the one removed before
   B. front of the file and remove the cards one at a time, placing each one face down on top of the one removed before
   C. back of the file and remove the cards in small groups, placing each group face down on top of the group removed before
   D. back of the file and remove the cards one at a time, placing each one face up on top of the one removed before

13. Assume you are the receptionist for Mr. Brown, an official in your department. It is your duty to permit only persons having important business to see this official; otherwise, you are to refer them to other members of the staff. A man tells you that he must see Mr. Brown on a very urgent and confidential matter. He gives you his name and says that Mr. Brown knows him, but he does not wish to tell you the nature of the matter. 13.____
Of the following, the BEST action for you to take under these circumstances is to

   A. permit this man to see Mr. Brown without further question, since the matter seems to be urgent
   B. refer this man to another member of the staff, since Mr. Brown may not wish to see him
   C. call Mr. Brown and explain the situation to him, and ask him whether he wishes to see this man
   D. tell this man that you will permit him to see Mr. Brown only if he informs you of the nature of his business

14. You are given copies of an important official notice together with a memorandum stating that each of the employees listed on the memorandum is to receive a copy of the official notice. 14.____
In order to have definite proof that each of the employees listed has received a copy of the notice, the BEST of the following courses of action for you to take as you hand the notice to each of the employees is to

   A. put your initials next to the employee's name on the memorandum
   B. ask the employee to sign the notice you have given him in your presence
   C. have the employee put his signature next to his name on the memorandum
   D. ask the employee to read the notice in your presence

15. The Mayor of the City of New York is elected for a term of _______ years. 15.____

A. 2 B. 3 C. 4 D. 5

KEY (CORRECT ANSWERS)

1. A
2. D
3. C
4. C
5. D
6. C
7. B
8. D
9. D
10. A
11. B
12. A
13. C
14. C
15. C

TEST 5

DIRECTIONS: Each question or incomplete statement is followed by several suggested answers or completions. Select the one that BEST answers the question or completes the statement. *PRINT THE LETTER OF THE CORRECT ANSWER IN THE SPACE AT THE RIGHT.*

1. When an employee is encouraged by his supervisor to think of new ideas in connection with his work, the habit of improving work methods is fostered. 1.____
   The one of the following which the MOST valid implication of the above statement is that

   A. the improvement of work methods should be the concern not only of the supervisor but of the employee as well
   B. an employee without initiative cannot perform his job well
   C. an employee may waste too much time in experimenting with new work methods
   D. an improved method for performing a task should not be used without the approval of the supervisor

2. The report on the work of the three employees furnishes definite proof that Jones is more efficient than Smith, and that Brown is less efficient than Jones. 2.____
   On the basis of the above information, the MOST accurate of the following statements is that

   A. Brown is more efficient than Smith
   B. Smith is more efficient than Brown
   C. Smith is not necessarily less efficient than Jones
   D. Brown is not necessarily more efficient than Smith

3. The Dewey Decimal System is used MOST widely in 3.____

   A. government offices
   B. private offices
   C. social welfare organizations
   D. libraries

4. Provision for handling a letter from a utility company marked *the first of next month* would necessitate that the letter be placed in a ______ file. 4.____

   A. follow-up
   B. numeric
   C. subject
   D. geographic

5. The SIMPLEST system of filing is 5.____

   A. subject
   B. geographic
   C. alphabetic
   D. numeric

6. Almost all students with a high school average of 80% or over were admitted to the college. 6.____
   On the basis of this statement, it would be MOST accurate to assume that

   A. a high school average of *80%* or over was required for admittance to the college
   B. some students with a high school average of less than 80% were admitted to the college
   C. a high school average of at least 80% was desirable but not necessary for admission to the college
   D. some students with a high school average of at least 80% were not admitted to the college

7. Suppose that you are filing a large number of cards. Your supervisor asks you to interrupt your work, arrange a group of letters alphabetically by name of writer, and then file the letters in a correspondence file. He asks, however, that you show the letters to him before you file them. You finish alphabetizing the letters in a few minutes, but your supervisor is not available. 7.____
Of the following, the BEST action for you to take is to

   A. file the letters as you have been directed, provided that your work has been checked by at least one other clerk
   B. file the letters as directed by your supervisor and explain to him when he returns the reason for your action
   C. wait at your supervisor's desk until he returns and you have an opportunity to show the letters to him
   D. resume filing cards until you have an opportunity to show the letters to your supervisor

8. The supervisor of a large central bureau is responsible for the accuracy of the work performed by her subordinates. The total number of errors made during the month indicates, in a general way, whether the work has been performed with reasonable accuracy. However, this is not in itself a true measure, but must be considered in relation to the total volume of work produced. 8.____
On the basis of this statement, the accuracy of work performed in a central typing bureau is MOST truly measured by the

   A. total number of errors made during a specified period
   B. comparison of the number of errors made during one month with the number made during the preceding month
   C. ratio between the number of errors made and the quantity of work produced during the month
   D. average amount of work produced by the unit during each month

9. As a clerk assigned to keeping payroll records in your department, you are instructed by your supervisor to use a new method for keeping the records. You think that the new method will be less effective than the one you are now using. 9.____
In this situation, it would be MOST advisable for you to

   A. use the new method to keep the records even if you think it may be less effective
   B. continue to use the method you consider to be more effective without saying anything to your supervisor
   C. use the method you consider to be more effective and then tell your supervisor your reasons for doing so
   D. use the new method only if you can improve its effectiveness

10. The term of office of a United States Senator is ______ years. 10.____

   A. 8 B. 6 C. 4 D. 2

11. Employees are required NOT to smoke in file rooms principally because 11.____

   A. they might interfere with the rights of others working in the same area
   B. of the danger of cancer
   C. of the narrow areas of the file room
   D. of the danger of fire

12. The MAIN reason a city employee should be polite is that 12.____

A. he may get into trouble if he is not polite
B. he never knows when he may be talking to a city official
C. politeness is a duty which any city employee owes the public
D. politeness will make him appear to be alert and efficient

13. In the United States, there is no 13.____

A. general sales tax
B. state income tax
C. state compulsory automobile inspection
D. state compulsory automobile insurance

14. It is LEAST correct to say that the commissioners of the various city departments are 14.____

A. appointed by the mayor and may usually be removed by him at will
B. generally part-time officials and serve without pay
C. responsible for submitting regular reports to the mayor on the operations of their departments
D. the top policy-making officials in these departments

15. The form of government under which the city of New York functions is known as the 15.____

A. Commision-Mayor
B. Council-Manager
C. Master-Plan
D. Mayor-Council

KEY (CORRECT ANSWERS)

1. A
2. D
3. D
4. A
5. D
6. D
7. D
8. C
9. A
10. B
11. D
12. C
13. A
14. B
15. D

EXAMINATION SECTION
TEST 1

DIRECTIONS: Each question or incomplete statement is followed by several suggested answers or completions. Select the one that BEST answers the question or completes the statement. *PRINT THE LETTER OF THE CORRECT ANSWER IN THE SPACE AT THE RIGHT.*

1. Suppose you have received dictation of several letters and have been given no specific instructions as to the order in which the material should be transcribed. So far as you can see, all of the letters are equally important. Which of the following is BEST to do? 1.____

   A. Transcribe the letters in the order in which they were dictated to you.
   B. Ask a more experienced co-worker for her opinion as to the order of transcription.
   C. Use your own judgment as to the order in which you should transcribe the letters.
   D. Ask your supervisor if he wishes you to type the letters in a particular order.

2. Suppose you are in a unit which has many incoming calls from the public. Your supervisor has given you the job of training newly appointed typists in techniques for answering the telephone. 2.____
   Of the following, which telephone response should be taught as the FIRST one to give upon picking up the telephone?

   A. Good morning. Who's calling, please?
   B. Who's this. Miss Smith speaking.
   C. Miss Smith. Who is this?
   D. Payroll Division. Miss Smith speaking.

3. You are in an office of 7 people. A woman calls your office, identifies herself as a client, and asks to speak to your supervisor, who is on another phone. 3.____
   What should you do in this situation? Ask her

   A. to hold until your supervisor is off the line
   B. to call back in ten minutes when you expect your supervisor to be free
   C. what she wants, to see if you or someone else can help her
   D. what she wants and, if you cannot help her, hang us

4. As the supervisor of a unit of stenographers, you have given a new employee an assignment which can easily be completed by, and which is needed by, the end of the day. She indicates some anxiety and says that she is not sure she can complete it in time. The other employees are very busy and unable to help. 4.____
   What should you do?

   A. Assign the stenographer to another task and finish the assignment yourself.
   B. Ask a supervisor from another unit if he could assign one of his workers to help your new stenographer.
   C. Tell the stenographer that right now is the time to conquer her anxiety by doing the job assigned to her.
   D. Review the assignment with the stenographer, check her progress, and be ready to help her when needed.

5. You supervise a stenographer who is writing many personal letters during work time while many of her assignments are not yet done. What should you do FIRST? 5.____

   A. Tell your supervisor that the stenographer needs more work since she is doing personal letters on the job.
   B. Make the stenographer stop personal work by telling her you will inform your supervisor unless she stops.
   C. Let the stenographer know that it is not proper to use government time for such personal projects.
   D. Give the stenographer enough work to keep her so busy that she won't be able to do personal work.

6. Suppose a stenographer working at an agency with equipment for transferring calls receives an outside call from someone who has reached the wrong extension. The stenographer knows the correct extension. The BEST thing for her to do in this case would be to 6.____

   A. signal the operator and tell him the extension to which to transfer the call
   B. give the caller the correct extension and offer to have him transferred to the correct extension
   C. give the person the correct extension and tell him to hang up and dial again
   D. tell the person he has reached the wrong extension and have him dial the operator

7. The supervisor in your office appears to be *dropping hints* about the condition of your desk. You feel that he may consider your desk somewhat sloppy. Which is the BEST way to handle this? 7.____

   A. Wait until your supervisor directly mentions your desk to you and then clean up.
   B. Straighten up your desk so that it can't be considered sloppy, and see if this stops the hints.
   C. Do nothing. Force your supervisor, by ignoring his hints, to stop *dropping the hints.*
   D. Tell the supervisor you have caught his hints and that now you would like him to speak his mind.

8. The instrument that should be used to write on a stencil is a 8.____

   A. stylus
   B. ballpoint pen
   C. paper clip
   D. pencil

9. A supervisor orienting a new stenographer advised her to be sure to note down in her notebook the date on which she took each piece of dictation. She told the stenographer to put the date on the same page as the dictated material. Which is the MOST important reason for dating the steno notebook? To 9.____

   A. know what date to put on the letters or reports the stenographer transcribes
   B. refer to these notes at a later date if necessary
   C. separate the letters from reports when transcribing them
   D. match incoming related correspondence to the material the stenographer transcribes

10. Assume you are in an office which uses a subject filing system. You find that frequently a letter to be filed involves two or three subjects. 10.____
In filing such a letter, it is MOST important to

A. file it under the subject that is mentioned first in the letter
B. prepare cross-references for the subjects covered in the letter
C. list all subjects involved on the label of the file folder
D. code the letter to show the main subject and its subdivisions

11. In addressing a letter to A.J. Brown, a commissioner in a governmental agency, the salutation that is considered MOST correct is: 11.____

A. Ms. or Mr. Brown:
B. Dear Commissioner Brown:
C. My dear Sir or Madam:
D. Commissioner Brown:

12. An office of a public agency frequently may need a number of copies of reports, forms, bulletins, letters, memos, and other kinds of written communications. 12.____
The particular type of duplicating process used to reproduce these copies does NOT usually depend on the

A. quality of work produced
B. number of copies required
C. cost of duplication
D. persons receiving the materials

13. A stenographer is transcribing a draft of a report from her notes. As soon as she transcribes a page of notes from her steno pad, she puts a line through that page. The MAIN reason for this procedure is that it 13.____

A. prevents grammatical errors in the report
B. prevents leaving out or repeating part of her notes
C. prevents making typographical errors from her notes
D. helps her to keep a count of the amount of work done

14. The MOST frequently used filing system in ordinary office practice is the ______ system. 14.____

A. alphabetic
B. numeric
C. geographic
D. subject

15. Your supervisor requests that you sign his name to, and mail, a letter he has dictated because he must leave to attend an important meeting. 15.____
In carrying out his request, you should remember to

A. sign your full name and title below the signature
B. imitate your superior's handwriting as closely as possible
C. type *Dictated but not read* in the lower left hand corner
D. add your initials next to or under the signature

16. Suppose a man speaking on the phone to you is having great difficulty making himself understood. He seems to be able to speak only in slang and cannot express himself easily. 16.____
What is the BEST thing to do to make sure you understand what he is saying?

A. Listen carefully, speak in your normal voice, and answer his questions as clearly as possible.
B. Use the same slang expressions and manner in which he speaks. This will give him confidence.
C. Let your irritation show in your voice so that he will *drop* his slang and speak more sensibly.
D. Ask your supervisor to answer his questions because the man's language is hard to understand.

17. There are few employees who do not seek meaning and some sort of challenge in their jobs. 17.____
Which of the following actions taken by a supervisor would BEST help to meet these needs?

A. Constantly reminding subordinates of the agency's high work expectations.
B. Explaining to subordinates how their work is related to that of other workers and how it contributes to agency objectives.
C. Telling employees that the longer the time needed to perform a job, the more important the job is.
D. Making it a policy to give each employee work which is slightly more difficult than his last assignment, but to explain such work carefully.

18. The one of the following over which a unit supervisor has the LEAST control is the _______ his unit. 18.____

A. quality of the work done in
B. nature of the work handled in
C. morale of workers in
D. increasing efficiency of

19. Suppose that you have received a note from an important official in your department commending the work of a unit of stenographers under your supervision. 19.____
Of the following, the BEST action for you to take is to

A. withhold the note for possible use at a time when the morale of the unit appears to be declining
B. show the note only to the better members of your staff as a reward for their good work
C. show the note only to the poorer members of your staff as a stimulus for better work
D. post the note conspicuously so that it can be seen by all members of your staff

20. If you find that one of your subordinates is becoming apathetic towards his work, you should 20.____

A. prefer charges against him
B. change the type of work
C. request his transfer
D. advise him to take a medical examination to check his health

21. Suppose that a new stenographer has been assigned to the unit which you supervise. To give this stenographer a brief picture of the functioning of your unit in the entire department would be 21.____

A. *commendable* because she will probably be able to perform her work with more understanding
B. *undesirable* because such action will probably serve only to confuse her
C. *commendable* because, if transferred, she would probably be able to work efficiently without additional training
D. *undesirable* because in-service training has been demonstrated to be less efficient than on-the-job training

22. Written instructions to a subordinate are of value because they 22.____

A. can be kept up-to-date
B. encourage initiative
C. make a job seem easier
D. are an aid in training

23. Suppose that you have assigned a task to a stenographer under your supervision and have given appropriate instructions. After a reasonable period, you check her work and find that one specific aspect of her work is consistently incorrect. 23.____
Of the following, the BEST action for you to take is to

A. determine whether the stenographer has correctly understood instructions concerning the aspect of the work not being done correctly
B. assign the task to a more competent stenographer
C. wait for the stenographer to commit a more flagrant error before taking up the matter with her
D. indicate to the stenographer that you are dissatisfied with her work and wait to see whether she is sufficiently intelligent to correct her own mistakes

24. If you wanted to check on the accuracy of the filing in your unit, you would 24.____

A. check all the files thoroughly at regular intervals
B. watch the clerks while they are filing
C. glance through filed papers at random
D. inspect thoroughly a small section of the files selected at random

25. In making job assignments to his subordinates, a supervisor should follow the principle that each individual GENERALLY is capable of 25.____

A. performing one type of work well and less capable of performing other types well
B. learning to perform a wide variety of different types of work
C. performing best the type of work in which he has had least experience
D. learning to perform any type of work in which he is given training

KEY (CORRECT ANSWERS)

1. D
2. D
3. C
4. D
5. C
6. B
7. B
8. A
9. B
10. B
11. B
12. D
13. B
14. A
15. D
16. A
17. C
18. B
19. D
20. B
21. A
22. D
23. A
24. D
25. B

TEST 2

DIRECTIONS: Each question or incomplete statement is followed by several suggested answers or completions. Select the one that BEST answers the question or completes the statement. *PRINT THE LETTER OF THE CORRECT ANSWER IN THE SPACE AT THE RIGHT.*

Questions 1-8.

DIRECTIONS: Questions 1 through 8 are to be answered on the basis of the RULES FOR ALPHABETICAL FILING given below. Read these rules carefully before answering the questions.

RULES FOR ALPHABETICAL FILING

Names of People

1. The names of people are filed in strict alphabetical order, first according to the last name, then according to first name or initial, and finally according to middle name or initial. For example: George Allen comes before Edward Bell, and Leonard P. Reston comes before Lucille Reston.

2. When last names are the same, for example, A. Green and Agnes Green, the one with the initial comes before the one with the name written out when the first initials are identical.

3. When first and last names are alike and the middle name is given, for example, John David Doe and John Devoe Doe, the names should be filed in alphabetical order of the middle names.

4. When first and last names are the same, a name without a middle initial comes before one with a middle name or initial. For example: John Doe comes before John A. Doe and John Alan Doe.

5. When first and last names are the same, a name with a middle initial comes before one with a middle name beginning with the same initial. For example: Jack R. Hertz comes before Jack Richard Hertz.

6. Prefixes such as De, O', Mac, Mc, and Van are filed as written and are treated as part of the names to which they are connected. For example: Robert O'Dea is filed before David Olsen.

7. Abbreviated names are treated as if they were spelled out. For example: Chas. is filed as Charles, and Thos. is filed as Thomas.

8. Titles and designations such as Dr., Mr., and Prof, are disregarded in filing.

Names of Organizations

1. The names of business organizations are filed according to the order in which each word in the name appears. When an organization name bears the name of a person, it is filed according to the rules for filing names of people as given above. For example: William Smith Service Co. comes before Television Distributors, Inc.

2. Where bureau, board, office, or department appears as the first part of the title of a governmental agency, that agency should be filed under the word in the title expressing the chief function of the agency. For example: Bureau of the Budget would be filed as if written Budget, (Bureau of the). The Department of Personnel would be filed as if written Personnel, (Department of).

3. When the following words are part of an organization, they are disregarded: the, of, and.

4. When there are numbers in a name, they are treated as if they were spelled out. For example: 10th Street Bootery is filed as Tenth Street Bootery.

Each of questions 1 through 8 contains four names numbered from I through IV, but not necessarily numbered in correct filing order. Answer each question by choosing the letter corresponding to the CORRECT filing order of the four names in accordance with the above rules.

Sample Question;

I. Robert J. Smith
II. R. Jeffrey Smith
III. Dr. A. Smythe
IV. Allen R. Smithers

A. I, II, III; IV
B. III, I, II, IV
C. II, I, IV, III
D. III, II, I, IV

Since the correct filing order, in accordance with the above rules, is II, I, IV, III, the CORRECT answer is C.

1. I. J. Chester VanClief 1.____
II. John C. VanClief
III. J. VanCleve
III. Mary L. Vance
The CORRECT answer is:

A. IV, III, I, II
B. IV, III, II, I
C. III, I, II, IV
D. III, IV, I, II

2. I. Community Development Agency 2.____
II. Department of Social Services
III. Board of Estimate
IV. Bureau of Gas and Electricity
The CORRECT answer is:

A. III, IV, I, II
B. I, II, IV, III
C. II, I, III, IV
D. I, III, IV, II

3. I. Dr. Chas. K. Dahlman 3.____
II. F. & A. Delivery Service
III. Department of Water Supply
IV. Demano Men's Custom Tailors
The CORRECT answer is:

A. I, II, III, IV
B. I, IV, II, III
C. IV, I, II, III
D. IV, I, III, II

4. I. 48th Street Theater 4.____
II. Fourteenth Street Day Care Center
III. Professor A. Cartwright
IV. Albert F. McCarthy
The CORRECT answer is:

A. IV, II, I, III
B. IV, III, I, II
C. III, II, I, IV
D. III, I, II, IV

5. I. Frances D'Arcy 5.____
II. Mario L. DelAmato
III. William R. Diamond
IV. Robert J. DuBarry
The CORRECT answer is:

A. I, II, IV, III
B. II, I, III, IV
C. I, II, III, IV
D. II, I, IV, III

6. I. Evelyn H. D'Amelio 6.____
II. Jane R. Bailey
III. J. Robert Bailey
IV. Frank Baily
The CORRECT answer is:

A. I, II, III, IV
B. I, III, II, IV
C. II, III, IV, I
D. III, II, IV, I

7. I. Department of Markets 7.____
II. Bureau of Handicapped Children
III. Housing Authority Administration Building
IV. Board of Pharmacy
The CORRECT answer is:

A. II, I, III, IV
B. I, II, IV, III
C. I, II, III, IV
D. III, II, I, IV

8. I. William A. Shea Stadium 8.____
II. Rapid Speed Taxi Co.
III. Harry Stampler's Rotisserie
IV. Wilhelm Albert Shea
The CORRECT answer is:

A. II, III, IV, I
B. IV, I, III, II
C. II, IV, I, III
D. III, IV, I, II

Questions 9-16.

DIRECTIONS: The employee identification codes in Column I begin and end with a capital letter and have an eight-digit number in between. In Questions 9 through 16, employee identification codes in Column I are to be arranged according to the following rules:

First: Arrange in alphabetical order according to the first letter.

Second: When two or more employee identification codes have the same first letter, arrange in alphabetical order according to the last letter.

Third: When two or more employee codes have the same first and last letters, arrange in numerical order, beginning with the lowest number.

The employee identification codes in Column I are numbered 1 through 5 in the order in which they are listed. In Column II, the numbers 1 through 5 are arranged in four different ways to show different arrangements of the corresponding employee identification numbers. Choose the answer in Column II in which the employee identification numbers are arranged according to the above rules.

Sample Question;

	Column I		Column II
1.	E75044127B	A.	4, 1, 3, 2, 5
2.	B96399104A	B.	4, 1, 2, 3, 5
3.	B93939086A	C.	4, 3, 2, 5, 1
4.	B47064465H	D.	3, 2, 5, 4, 1
5.	B99040922A		

In the sample question, the four employee identification codes starting with B should be put before the employee identification code starting with E. The employee identification codes starting with B and ending with A should be put before the employee identification codes starting with B and ending with H. The three employee identification codes starting with B and ending with A should be listed in numerical order, beginning with the lowest number. The correct way to arrange the employee identification codes, therefore, is 3, 2, 5, 4, 1, shown below.

3. B93939086A
2. B96399104A
5. B99040922A
4. B47064465H
1. E75044127B

Therefore, the answer to the sample question is D.

		Column I	Column II	
9.	1.	G42786441J	A. 2, 5, 4, 3, 1	9.____
	2.	H45665413J	B. 5, 4, 1, 3, 2	
	3.	G43117690J	C. 4, 5, 1, 3, 2	
	4.	G43546698I	D. 1, 3, 5, 4, 2	
	5.	G41679942I		
10.	1.	S44556178T	A. 1, 3, 5, 2, 4	10.____
	2.	T43457169T	B. 4, 3, 5, 2, 1	
	3.	S53321176T	C. 5, 3, 1, 2, 4	
	4.	T53317998S	D. 5, 1, 3, 4, 2	
	5.	S67673942S		
11.	1.	R63394217D	A. 5, 4, 2, 3, 1	11.____
	2.	R63931247D	B. 1, 5, 3, 2, 4	
	3.	R53931247D	C. 5, 3, 1, 2, 4	
	4.	R66874239D	D. 5, 1, 2, 3, 4	
	5.	R46799366D		
12.	1.	A35671968B	A. 3, 2, 1, 4, 5	12.____
	2.	A35421794C	B. 2, 3, 1, 5, 4	
	3.	A35466987B	C. 1, 3 , 2, 4, 5	
	4.	C10435779A	D. 3, 1, 2, 4, 5	
	5.	C00634779B		
13.	1.	I99746426Q	A. 2, 1, 3, 5, 4	13.____
	2.	I10445311Q	B. 5, 4, 2, 1, 3	
	3.	J63749877P	C. 4, 5, 3, 2, 1	
	4.	J03421739Q	D. 2, 1, 4, 5, 3	
	5.	J00765311Q		
14.	1.	M33964217N	A. 4, 1, 5, 2, 3	14.____
	2.	N33942770N	B. 5, 1, 4, 3, 2	
	3.	N06155881M	C. 4, 1, 5, 3, 2	
	4.	M00433669M	D. 1, 4, 5, 2, 3	
	5.	M79034577N		
15.	1.	D77643905C	A. 1, 2, 5, 3, 4	15.____
	2.	D44106788C	B. 5, 3, 2, 1, 4	
	3.	D13976022F	C. 2, 1, 5, 3, 4	
	4.	D97655430E	D. 2, 1, 4, 5, 3	
	5.	D00439776F		
16.	1.	W22746920A	A. 2, 1, 3, 4, 5	16.____
	2.	W22743720A	B. 2, 1, 5, 3, 4	
	3.	W32987655A	C. 1, 2, 3, 4, 5	
	4.	W43298765A	D. 1, 2, 5, 3, 4	
	5.	W30987433A		

Questions 17-22.

DIRECTIONS: Questions 17 through 22 are to be answered on the basis of the information given in the chart below. This chart shows the results of a study made of the tasks performed by a stenographer during one day. Included in the chart are the time at which she started a certain task and, under the particular task heading, the amount of time, in minutes, she took to complete the task, and explanations of telephone calls and miscellaneous activities.

NOTE: The time spent at lunch should not be included in any of your calculations.

PAMELA JOB STUDY

NAME: Pamela Donald DATE: 9/26
JOB TITLE: Stenographer
DIVISION: Stenographic Pool

Time of Start of Task	TASKS PERFORMED						Explanations of Telephone Calls and Miscellaneous Activities
	Taking Dictation	Typing	Filing	Telephone Work	Handling Mail	Misc. Activities	
9:00					22		
9:22						13	Picking up supplies
9:35						15	Cleaning typewriter
9:50	11						
10:01		30					
10:31				8			Call to Agency A
10:39	12						
10:51			10				
11 : 01				7			Call from Agency B
11:08		30					
11:38	10						
11:48				12			Call from Agency C
12:00	L U N C H						
1:00					28		
1 : 28	13						
1:41		32					
2:13				12			Call to Agency B
X			15				
Y		50					
3:30	10						
3:40			21				
4:01				9			Call from Agency A
4:10	35						
4:45		9					
4:54						6	Cleaning up desk

Sample Question;

The total amount of time spent on miscellaneous activities in the morning is exactly equal to the total amount of time spent

A. filing in the morning
B. handling mail in the afternoon
C. miscellaneous activities in the afternoon
D. handling mail in the morning

Explanation of answer to sample question:

The total amount of time spent on miscellaneous activities in the morning equals 28 minutes (13 minutes for picking up supplies plus 15 minutes for cleaning the typewriter); and since it takes 28 minutes to handle mail in the afternoon, the answer is B.

17. The time labeled Y at which the stenographer started a typing assignment was 17.____

A. 2:15 B. 2:25 C. 2:40 D. 2:50

18. The ratio of time spent on all incoming calls to time spent on all outgoing calls for the day was 18.____

A. 5:7 B. 5:12 C. 7:5 D. 7:12

19. Of the following combinations of tasks, which ones take up exactly 80% of the total time spent on *Tasks Performed* during the day? 19.____

A. Typing, filing, telephone work, and handling mail
B. Taking dictation, filing, and miscellaneous activities
C. Taking dictation, typing, handling mail, and miscellaneous activities
D. Taking dictation, typing, filing, and telephone work

20. The total amount of time spent transcribing or typing work is how much more than the total amount of time spent in taking dictation? 20.____

A. 55 minutes B. 1 hour
C. 1 hour 10 minutes D. 1 hour 25 minutes

21. The GREATEST number of shifts in activities occurred between the times of 21.____

A. 9:00 A.M. and 10:31 A.M.
B. 9:35 A.M. and 11:01 A.M.
C. 10:31 A.M. and 12:00 Noon
D. 3:30 P.M. and 5:00 P.M.

22. The total amount of time spent on taking dictation in the morning plus the total amount of time spent on filing in the afternoon is exactly equal to the total amount of time spent on 22.____

A. typing in the afternoon minus the total amount of time spent on telephone work in the afternoon
B. typing in the morning plus the total amount of time spent on miscellaneous activities in the afternoon
C. dictation in the afternoon plus the total amount of time spent on filing in the morning

D. typing in the afternoon minus the total amount of time spent on handling mail in the morning

Questions 23-30.

DIRECTIONS: Each of Questions 23 through 30 consists of a set of letters and numbers. For each question, pick as your answer from the column to the right the choice which has ONLY numbers and letters that are in the question you are answering.

Sample Question:

B-9-P-H-2-Z-N-8-4-M

A. B-4-C-3-H-9
B. 4-H-P-8-6-N
C. P-2-Z-8-M-9
D. 4-B-N-5-E-2

Choice C is the correct answer because P, 2, Z, 8, M, 9 are in the sample question. All the other choices have at least one letter or number that is not in the question.

Questions 23 through 26 are based on Column I.
Questions 27 through 30 are based on Column II.

Column I

23. X-8-3-I-H-9-4-G-P-U — A. I-G-W-8-2-1 — 23.____
24. 4-1-2-X-U-B-9-H-7-3 — B. U-3-G-9-P-8 — 24.____
25. U-I-G-2-5-4-W-P-3-8 — C. 3-G-I-4-8-U — 25.____
26. 3-H-7-G-4-5-I-U-8 — D. 9-X-4-7-2-H — 26.____

Column II

27. L-2-9-Z-R-8-Q-Y-5-7 — A. 8-R-N-3-T-Z — 27.____
28. J-L-9-N-Y-8-5-Q-Z-2 — B. 2-L-R-5-7-Q — 28.____
29. T-Y-8-3-J-Q-2-N-R-Z — C. J-2-8-Z-Y-5 — 29.____
30. 8-Z-7-T-N-L-1-E-R-3 — D. Z-8-9-3-L-5 — 30.____

KEY (CORRECT ANSWERS)

1. A
2. D
3. B
4. D
5. C

6. D
7. D
8. C
9. B
10. D

11. C
12. D
13. A
14. C
15. D

16. B
17. C
18. C
19. D
20. B

21. C
22. D
23. B
24. D
25. C

26. C
27. B
28. C
29. A
30. A

TEST 3

DIRECTIONS: Each question or incomplete statement is followed by several suggested answers or completions. Select the one that BEST answers the question or completes the statement. *PRINT THE LETTER OF THE CORRECT ANSWER IN THE SPACE AT THE RIGHT.*

Questions 1-6.

DIRECTIONS: In Questions 1 through 6, only one of the sentences lettered A, B, C, or D is grammatically correct. Pick as your answer the sentence that is CORRECT from the point of view of grammar when used in formal correspondence.

1. A. There is four tests left. 1.____
   B. The number of tests left are four.
   C. There are four tests left.
   D. Four of the tests remains.

2. A. Each of the applicants takes a test. 2.____
   B. Each of the applicants take a test.
   C. Each of the applicants take tests.
   D. Each of the applicants have taken tests.

3. A. The applicant, not the examiners, are ready. 3.____
   B. The applicants, not the examiner, is ready.
   C. The applicants, not the examiner, are ready.
   D. The applicant, not the examiner, are ready.

4. A. You will not progress except you practice. 4.____
   B. You will not progress without you practicing.
   C. You will not progress unless you practice.
   D. You will not progress provided you do not practice.

5. A. Neither the director or the employees will be at the office tomorrow. 5.____
   B. Neither the director nor the employees will be at the office tomorrow.
   C. Neither the director, or the secretary nor the other employees will be at the office tomorrow.
   D. Neither the director, the secretary or the other employees will be at the office tomorrow.

6. A. In my absence he and her will have to finish the assignment. 6.____
   B. In my absence,he and she will have to finish the assignment.
   C. In my absence she and him, they will have to finish the assignment.
   D. In my absence he and her both will have to finish the assignment.

Questions 7-12.

DIRECTIONS: Questions 7 through 12 consist of a sentence lacking certain needed punctuation. Pick as your answer the description of punctuation which will CORRECTLY complete the sentence.

7. If you take the time to keep up your daily correspondence you will no doubt be most efficient. Comma(s) 7.____

   A. only after *doubt*
   B. only after *correspondence*
   C. after *correspondence, will,* and *be*
   D. after *if, correspondence,* and *will*

8. Because he did not send the application soon enough he did not receive the up to date copy of the book. Comma(s) 8.____

   A. after *application* and *enough,* and quotation marks before *up* and after *date*
   B. after *application* and *enough,* and hyphens between *to* and *date*
   C. after *enough,* and hyphens between *up* and *to* and between *to* and *date*
   D. after *application,* and quotation marks before *up* and after *date*

9. The coordinator requested from the department the following items a letter each week summarizing progress personal forms and completed applications for tests. 9.____

   A. Commas after *items* and *completed*
   B. Semi-colon after *items* and *progress,* comma after *forms*
   C. Colon after *items,* commas after *progress* and *forms*
   D. Colon after *items,* commas after *forms* and *applications*

10. The supervisor asked Who will attend the conference next month 10.____

   A. Comma after *asked,* period after *month*
   B. Period after *asked,* question mark after *month*
   C. Comma after *asked,* quotation marks before *Who,* quotation marks after *month,* and question mark after the quotation marks
   D. Comma after *asked,* quotation marks before *Who,* question mark after *month,* and quotation marks after the question mark

11. When the statistics are collected we will forward the results to you as soon as possible. Comma(s) after 11.____

   A. *you*
   B. *forward* and *you*
   C. *collected, results,* and *you*
   D. *collected*

12. The ecology of our environment is concerned with mans pollution of the atmosphere. 12.____

   A. Comma after *ecology*
   B. Apostrophe after *n* and before *s* in *mans*
   C. Commas after *ecology* and *environment*
   D. Apostrophe after *s* in *mans*

Questions 13-18.

DIRECTIONS: Each of Questions 13 through 18 consists of three words. In each question, one of the words may be spelled incorrectly or all three words may be spelled correctly. If one of the words in a question is spelled incorrectly, indicate in the space at the right the letter preceding the word which is spelled incorrectly. If all three words are spelled correctly, print in the space at the right the letter D.

13. A. sincerely B. affectionately C. truly 13.____

14. A. excellant B. verify C. important 14.____

15. A. error B. quality C. enviroment 15.____

16. A. exercise B. advance C. pressure 16.____

17. A. citizen B. expence C. memory 17.____

18. A. flexable B. focus C. forward 18.____

19. A senior stenographer earned $40,200 a year and had 4.5% state tax withheld for the year 2016. 19.____
If she was paid every two weeks, the amount of state tax that was taken out of each of her paychecks, based on a 52-week year, was MOST NEARLY

A. $62.76 B. $64.98 C. $69.54 D. $73.98

20. Two stenographers have been assigned to address 750 envelopes. One stenographer addresses twice as many envelopes per hour as the other stenographer. 20.____
If it takes five hours for them to complete the job, the rate of the slower stenographer is _______ envelopes per hour.

A. 35 B. 50 C. 75 D. 100

21. Suppose that the postage rate for mailing single copies of a magazine to persons not included on a subscription list is 60 cents for the first two ounces of the single copy and 10 cents for each additional ounce. 21.____
If 19 copies of a magazine, each of which weighs eleven ounces, are mailed to 19 different people, the TOTAL postage cost of these magazines is

A. $11.40 B. $13.30 C. $20.90 D. $28.50

22. A senior stenographer spends about 40 hours a month taking dictation. Of that time, 44% is spent taking minutes of meetings, 38% is spent taking dictation of lengthy reports, and the rest of the time is spent taking dictation of letters and memoranda. 22.____
How much MORE time is spent taking minutes of meetings than in taking dictation of letters and memoranda?
10 hours ______minutes

A. 6 B. 16 C. 24 D. 40

23. In one week, a stenographer typed 65 letters. Forty letters had 4 copies on onion skin. The rest had 3 copies on onion skin. 23.____
If the stenographer had 500 sheets of onion skin on hand at the beginning of the week when she started typing the letters, how many sheets of onion skin did she have left at the end of the week?

A. 190 B. 235 C. 265 D. 305

24. An agency is planning to microfilm letters and other correspondence of the last five years. The number of letter size documents that can be photographed on a 100-foot roll of microfilm is 2,995. The agency estimates that it will need 240 feet of microfilm to do all the pages of all of the letters. 24.____
How many pages of letter size documents can be photographed on this microfilm?

A. 5,990 B. 6,786 C. 7,188 D. 7,985

25. In an agency, 2/3 of the total number of female stenographers and 1/2 of the total number of male stenographers attended a general staff meeting. 25.____
If there are a total of 56 stenographers in the agency and 25% of them are male, the number of female stenographers who attended the general staff meeting is

A. 14 B. 28 C. 36 D. 42

26. A worker is currently earning $42,850 a year and pays $875 a month for rent. He expects to get a raise that will enable him to move into an apartment where his rent will be 25% of his new yearly salary. 26.____
If this new apartment is going to cost him $975 a month, what is the TOTAL amount of raise that he expects to get?

A. $1,200 B. $2,450 C. $3,950 D. $4,600

27. The tops of five desks in an office are to be covered with a scratch-resistant material. Each desk top measures 60 inches by 36 inches. 27.____
How many square feet of material will be needed for the five desk tops?

A. 15 B. 75 C. 96 D. 180

Questions 28-33.

DIRECTIONS: Questions 28 through 33 test how well you understand what you read. It will be necessary for you to read carefully because your answers to these questions should be based ONLY on the information given in the following passage.

Years ago, senior stenographers needed to understand the basic operations of data processing. On punched cards, magnetic tape or on other media, data was recorded before being fed into the computer for processing. A machine such as the keypunch was used to convert the data written on the source document into the coded symbols on punched cards or tapes. After data was converted, it was verified to guarantee absolute accuracy of conversion. In this manner, data became a permanent record that can be read by electronic computers.

Today, senior stenographers enter similar data directly into computer systems using word-processing, spreadsheet, publishing and other types of software. Rather than concern themselves with symbols and conversions, stenographers can transcribe information in programs like Microsoft Word or Google Docs, and enter numerical information into Microsoft Excel, which can then create charts and formulas out of that basic data.

28. Of the following, the BEST title for the above passage is: 28.____

A. THE STENOGRAPHER AS DATA PROCESSOR
B. THE RELATION OF KEYPUNCHING TO STENOGRAPHY
C. THE EVOLUTION OF DATA PROCESSING
D. PERMANENT OFFICE RECORDS

29. According to the above passage, the role of the senior stenographer is different in the present day in that 29.____

A. data can be entered directly into computer programs
B. it requires knowledge of multiple methods of recording data
C. ultimately, all data winds up being recorded on a computer
D. stenographers must have an advanced understanding of software and programming

30. Based on the passage, which of the following is NOT an example of a task a senior stenographer would carry out today? 30.____

A. Entering text into a pamphlet using publishing software
B. Recording sales figures and sending them to a programmer for processing
C. Recording purchasing data in an Excel spreadsheet
D. Typing an orally dictated draft in a Word document

31. According to the above passage, computers are used MOST often to handle 31.____

A. management data
B. problems of higher education
C. the control of chemical processes
D. payroll operations

32. Computer programming is taught in many colleges and business schools. The above passage IMPLIES that programmers in industry 32.____

A. must have professional training
B. need professional training to advance
C. must have at least a college education to do adequate programming tasks
D. do not need college education to do programming work

33. According to the above passage, data to be processed by computer should be 33.____

A. recent B. complete C. basic D. verified

Questions 34-40.

DIRECTIONS: In each of the following groups of sentences, one of the four sentences is faulty in grammar, punctuation, or capitalization. Select the INCORRECT sentence in each case.

34. A. If you had stood at home and done your homework, you would not have failed in arithmetic. 34.____
B. Her affected manner annoyed every member of the audience.
C. How will the new law affect our income taxes?
D. The plants were not affected by the long, cold winter, but they succumbed to the drought of summer.

35. A. He is one of the most able men who have been in the Senate. 35.____
B. It is he who is to blame for the lamentable mistake.
C. Haven't you a helpful suggestion to make at this time?
D. The money was robbed from the blind man's cup.

36. A. The amount of children in this school is steadily increasing. 36.____
B. After taking an apple from the table, she went out to play.
C. He borrowed a dollar from me.
D. I had hoped my brother would arrive before me.

37. A. Whom do you think I hear from every week? 37.____
B. Who do you think is the right man for the job?
C. Who do you think I found in the room?
D. He is the man whom we considered a good candidate for the presidency.

38. A. Quietly the puppy laid down before the fireplace. 38.____
B. You have made your bed; now lie in it.
C. I was badly sunburned because I had lain too long in the sun.
D. I laid the doll on the bed and left the room.

39. A. Sailing down the bay was a thrilling experience for me. 39.____
B. He was not consulted about your joining the club.
C. This story is different than the one I told you yesterday.
D. There is no doubt about his being the best player.

40. A. He maintains there is but one road to world peace. 40.____
B. It is common knowledge that a child sees much he is not supposed to see.
C. Much of the bitterness might have been avoided if arbitration had been resorted to earlier in the meeting.
D. The man decided it would be advisable to marry a girl somewhat younger than him.

KEY (CORRECT ANSWERS)

1.	C	21.	D
2.	A	22.	C
3.	C	23.	C
4.	C	24.	C
5.	B	25.	B
6.	B	26.	C
7.	B	27.	B
8.	C	28.	C
9.	C	29.	A
10.	D	30.	B
11.	D	31.	A
12.	B	32.	D
13.	D	33.	D
14.	A	34.	A
15.	C	35.	D
16.	D	36.	A
17.	B	37.	C
18.	A	38.	A
19.	C	39.	C
20.	B	40.	D

EXAMINATION SECTION

DIRECTIONS: Each question or incomplete statement is followed by several suggested answers or completions. Select the one that BEST answers the question or completes the statement. *PRINT THE LETTER OF THE CORRECT ANSWER IN THE SPACE AT THE RIGHT.*

Questions 1-15:
For each of the following questions, PRINT on the space at the right the word TRUE if the statement is true, or FALSE if the statement is false.

1. A typist who discovers an obvious grammatical error in a report she is typing should, under ordinary circumstances, copy the material as it was given to her. 1.______

2. The initials of the typist who typed a business letter generally appear on the letter. 2.______

3. It is considered POOR letter form to have *only* the complimentary close and the signature on the second page of a business letter. 3.______

4. Correspondence which is filed according to dates of letters is said to be filed chronologically. 4.______

5. It is *usually* unnecessary to proofread punctuation marks in a report. 5.______

6. The use of window envelopes *reduces* probability of mailing a letter to the wrong address. 6.______

7. Letter size paper is *usually* longer than legal size paper. 7.______

8. It is considered GOOD typing form to have two spaces following a comma. 8.______

9. Both sheets of a two-page typed letter MUST be letterheads. 9.______

10. Before removing a typed letter from the typewriter, the typist should read the copy so that corrections may be made neatly. 10.______

11. When alphabetizing names, you should ALWAYS disregard first names. 11.______

12. When filing a large number of cards according to the name on each card, it is generally a *good* procedure to alphabetize the cards FIRST. 12.______

13. When a report may be filed in a subject file under two headings, it is *good* practice to make a cross reference. 13.______

14. If an essential point has been omitted in a business letter, it is usually considered *good* letter form to include this point in a brief postscript. 14.______

15. Rough draft copies of a report should generally be single-spaced. 15.______

Questions 16-22:
The following items consist of problems in arithmetic. Print in the space at the right the word TRUE if the statement is true, and FALSE if the statement is false.

16. If the rate for first-class mail is 37 cents for each ounce or fraction of an ounce and 23 cents for each ounce or fraction of an ounce above one ounce, then the total cost of sending by first-class mail three letters weighing 1-1/2 ounces, 2 ounces, and 2-1/2 ounces, respectively, would be $1.80. 16.______

17. A typist, who in one hour typed a report consisting of five pages with 60 lines per page and 10 words per line, would have typed at the rate of 45 words per minute. 17.______

18. If a department store employs 45 clerks, 21 typists, and 18 stenographers, the percentage of these employees who are typists is 25%. 18.______

19. If four typists, who type at the same rate of speed, type 1,000 letters in 12 hours, then it will take six typists nine hours to type 1,000 letters. 19.______

20. If 15% of a stenographer's time is spent in taking dictation and 45% of her time is taken up in transcribing her notes, then she has a remainder of two-fifths of her time for performing other duties. 20.______

21. A typist completed 14 pages of a 24-page report before being asked to speak briefly with her employer, then typed the remaining 10 pages. Up until the time she spoke with her employer, the typist had already completed approximately 58% of the report. 21.______

22. Employee A types at a rate of 48 words per minute, while Employee B types at a rate of 54 words per minute. If both employees spend exactly 2-1/4 hours typing reports, Employee B will have typed approximately 810 more words than Employee A. 22.______

Questions 23-54:
Each of the following items consists of two words preceded by the letters A and B. In each item, *one* of the words may be spelled INCORRECTLY, or *both* words may be spelled CORRECTLY. If one of the words is spelled incorrectly, print in the space at the right the letter corresponding to the incorrect word. If both are spelled correctly, print the answer C.

23. A. accessible B. artifical 23.______

24. A. feild B. arranged 24.______

25. A. admittence B. hastily 25.______

26. A. easely B. readily 26.______

27. A. pursue B. decend 27.______

28. A. measure B. laboratory 28.______

29. A. exausted B. traffic 29.______

30. A. discussion B. unpleasant 30.______

31. A. campaign B. murmer 31.______

32. A. guarantee B. sanatary 32.______

33. A. communication B. safty 33.______

34. A. numerus B. celebration 34.______

35. A. nourish B. begining 35.______

36. A. courious B. witness 36.______

37. A. undoubtedly B. thoroughly 37.______

38. A. justified B. offering 38.______

39. A. predjudice B. license 39.______

40. A. label B. pamphlet 40.______

41. A. bulletin B. physical 41.______

42. A. assure B. exceed 42.______

43. A. advantagous B. evident 43.______

44. A. benefit B. occured 44. ______

45. A. acquire B. graditude 45. ______

46. A. amenable B. boundry 46. ______

47. A. deceive B. voluntary 47. ______

48. A. imunity B. conciliate 48. ______

49. A. acknoledge B. presume 49. ______

50. A. substitute B. prespiration 50. ______

51. A. reputible B. announce 51. ______

52. A. luncheon B. wretched 52. ______

53. A. regrettable B. proficiency 53. ______

54. A. rescind B. dissappoint 54. ______

Questions 55-72:
Each of the sentences that follow may be classified MOST appropriately under one of the following three categories:

A. *faulty* because of incorrect grammar
B. *faulty* because of incorrect punctuation
C. *correct*

Examine each sentence, then select the best answer as listed above and place the letter in the space at the right. All incorrect sentences contain only ONE type of error. Consider a sentence correct if it contains none of the types of errors mentioned, even though there may be other correct ways of expressing the same thought.

55. He sent the notice to the clerk who hired you yesterday. 55. ______

56. It must be admitted, however that you were not informed of this change. 56. ______

57. Only the employees who have served in this grade for at least two years are eligible for promotion. 57. ______

58. The work was divided equally between she and Mary. 58. ______

59. He thought that you were not available at the time. 59. ______

60. When the messenger returns; please give him this package. 60. ______

61. The new secretary prepared, typed, addressed, and delivered, the notices. 61. ______

62. Walking into the room, his desk can be seen at the rear. 62. ______

63. Although John has worked here longer then she, he produces a smaller amount of work. 63. ______

64. She said she could of typed this report yesterday. 64. ______

65. Neither one of these procedures are adequate for the efficient performance of this task. 65. ______

66. The typewriter is the tool of the typist; the cash register, the tool of the cashier. 66. ______

67. "The assignment must be completed as soon as possible" said the supervisor. 67. ______

68. As you know, office handbooks are issued to all new employees. 68. ______

69. Writing a speech is sometimes easier than to deliver it before an audience. 69. ______

70. Mr. Brown our accountant, will audit the accounts next week. 70. ______

71. Give the assignment to whomever is able to do it most efficiently. 71. ______

72. The supervisor expected either your or I to file these reports. 72. ______

Questions 73-90:
For each of the following test items, print the letter in the space at the right of the answer that BEST completes the statement.

73. A PREVALENT practice is one which is 73. ______
A. rare B. unfair C. widespread D. correct

74. To prepare a RECAPITULATION means *most nearly* to prepare a 74. ______
A. summary B. revision C. defense D. decision

75. An ADVERSE decision is one which is 75. ______
A. unfavorable B. unwise
C. anticipated D. backwards

76. A COMMENDATORY report is one which 76. ______
A. expresses praise B. contains contradictions
C. is too detailed D. is threatening

77. "The council will DEFER action on this matter." The word DEFER means *most nearly* 77. ______
A. hasten B. consider C. postpone D. reject

78. MEAGER results are those which are 78. ______
A. satisfactory B. scant
C. unexpected D. praiseworthy

79. An ARDUOUS job assignment 79. ______
A. requires much supervision B. is laborious
C. absorbs one's interest D. is lengthy

80. "This employee was IMPLICATED." The word IMPLICATED *most nearly* means 80. ______
A. demoted B. condemned C. involved D. accused

81. To be DETAINED means *most nearly* to be 81. ______
A. entertained B. held back
C. sent away D. scolded

82. An AMIABLE person is one who is 82. ______
A. active B. pleasing C. thrifty D. foolish

83. A UNIQUE procedure is one which is 83. ______
A. simple B. uncommon C. useless D. ridiculous

84. The word REPLENISH means *most nearly* to 84. ______
A. give up B. punish C. refill D. empty

85. A CONCISE report is one which is 85. ______
A. logical B. favorable C. brief D. intelligent

86. ELATED means *most nearly* 86. ______
A. lengthened B. matured C. excited D. youthful

87. SANCTION means *most nearly* 87. ______
A. approval B. delay C. priority D. veto

88. EGOTISTIC means *most nearly* 88. ______
A. tiresome B. self-centered
C. sly D. smartly attired

89. TRITE means *most nearly* 89. ______
A. brilliant B. unusual
C. funny D. commonplace

90. FESTIVE means *most nearly* 90. ______
A. edible B. joyous C. proud D. serene

KEY (CORRECT ANSWERS)

1. F	31. B	61. B
2. T	32. B	62. A
3. T	33. B	63. C
4. T	34. A	64. A
5. F	35. B	65. A
6. T	36. A	66. C
7. F	37. C	67. B
8. F	38. C	68. C
9. F	39. A	69. A
10. T	40. C	70. B
11. F	41. C	71. A
12. T	42. C	72. A
13. T	43. A	73. C
14. F	44. B	74. A
15. F	45. B	75. A
16. F	46. B	76. A
17. F	47. C	77. C
18. T	48. A	78. B
19. F	49. A	79. B
20. T	50. B	80. C
21. T	51. A	81. B
22. T	52. C	82. B
23. B	53. C	83. B
24. A	54. B	84. C
25. A	55. A	85. C
26. A	56. B	86. C
27. B	57. C	87. A
28. C	58. A	88. B
29. A	59. C	89. D
30. C	60. B	90. B

EXAMINATION SECTION
TEST 1

DIRECTIONS: Below are 10 groups of statements and conclusions, numbered 1 through 10. For each group of statements, select the one conclusion lettered A, B, C, which is fully supported by and is based SOLELY on the statements. *PRINT THE LETTER OF THE CORRECT ANSWER IN THE SPACE AT THE RIGHT.*

1. He is either approved or disapproved for this examination. But, he is not approved. Therefore, he is 1.____

   A. qualified B. disapproved C. a taxpayer

2. In planning the itinerary for Mr. Kane, his secretary told him: Route 20 runs parallel to Route 6. Route 6 runs parallel to Route 18. 2.____
   Mr. Kane concluded that,
   Therefore, Route

   A. 20 is north of Route 6
   B. 18 intersects Route 20
   C. 20 is parallel to Route 18

3. Either the valedictorian is more intelligent than the salutatorian, or as intelligent, or less intelligent. 3.____
   But the valedictorian is not more intelligent, nor is she less intelligent.
   Therefore, the valedictorian is

   A. less intelligent than the salutatorian
   B. as intelligent as the salutatorian
   C. more intelligent than the salutatorian

4. If the date for the examination is changed, it will be held July 28, or it will be postponed until October 15. 4.____
   The date is not changed.
   Therefore, the examination

   A. will probably be held July 28
   B. date is uncertain
   C. will be held July 28, or it will be postponed until October 15

5. Joan transcribes faster than Nancy. 5.____
   Nancy transcribes faster than Anne.
   Therefore,

   A. Nancy transcribes faster than Joan
   B. Joan transcribes faster than Anne
   C. Nancy has had longer experience than Anne in taking dictation

6. The files in Division D contain either pending matter, completed case records, or dead material. 6.____
   They do not contain pending matter.
   Therefore, they contain

A. completed case records
B. completed case records and dead material
C. either completed case records or dead material

7. Either stenographer B in pool C types faster than stenographer A in pool D, or she types at the same rate as stenographer A, or she types slower than stenographer A. But, she does not type faster than stenographer A, nor does she type slower than stenographer Therefore, stenographer 7.____

A. B does not type as fast as stenographer A
B. B is more efficient than stenographer A
C. A types as fast as stenographer B

8. Miss Andre can be eligible for retirement when she has been in city service 35 years, or if she is 55 years of age. She is fifty-four years old and has been in city service 36 years. Therefore, she 8.____

A. is not eligible for retirement now
B. is eligible for retirement now
C. will be eligible for retirement only if she stays in city service for another year

9. If K is L, O is P; if M is N, Q is R. 9.____
Either K is L, or M is N.
Therefore,

A. K is P or M is R
B. either O is P or Q is R
C. the conclusion is uncertain

10. If the employee is in error, the supervisor's refusal to listen to his side is unreasonable. If he is not in error, the supervisor's refusal is unjust. But the employee is in error or he is not. 10.____
Therefore, the supervisor's refusal

A. may be considered later
B. is either unreasonable or it is unjust
C. is justifiable

KEY (CORRECT ANSWERS)

1.	B	6.	C
2.	C	7.	C
3.	B	8.	B
4.	B	9.	B
5.	B	10.	B

TEST 2

Questions 1-5

DIRECTIONS: Below are 5 groups of statements and conclusions, numbered 1 through 5. For each group of statements, select the one conclusion lettered A, B, C, which is fully supported by and is based SOLELY on the statements. *PRINT THE LETTER OF THE CORRECT ANSWER IN THE SPACE AT THE RIGHT.*

1. Three desks are placed in a straight row just inside the door in our office. Desk 1 is farther from the door than Desk 2. Desk 3 is farther from the door than Desk 1. Which desk is in the middle position from the door? Desk 1.____

   A. 1 B. 2 C. 3

2. The problem is either correct or incorrect or is unsolvable. The problem is not correct. Therefore, the 2.____

   A. problem is incorrect
   B. problem is either incorrect or is unsolvable
   C. conclusion is uncertain

3. Village E is situated between City F and Village G. City F is situated between Village G and Town H. Therefore, Village E is 3.____

   A. not situated between Village G and Town H
   B. situated between City F and Town H
   C. situated nearer to City F than to Town H

4. Jurisdiction No. 1 is between Jurisdictions No. 2 and No. 3. Jurisdiction No. 2 is between Jurisdictions No. 3 and No. 4. Therefore, Jurisdiction No. 1 is 4.____

   A. not between Jurisdictions No. 3 and No. 4
   B. between Jurisdictions No. 2 and No. 4
   C. nearer to Jurisdiction No. 2 than to No. 4

5. Five candidates (A, B, C, D, and E) are seated in the same room. D is between A and B, E is between A and D. C is the same distance from A and E, and D is the same distance from A and B. Therefore, 5.____

   A. E is nearer to B than to A
   B. C is nearer to E than to D
   C. B is nearer to E than to D

Questions 6-10.

DIRECTIONS: Each question or incomplete statement is followed by several suggested answers or completions. Select the one that BEST answers the question or completes the statement. *PRINT THE LETTER OF THE CORRECT ANSWER IN THE SPACE AT THE RIGHT.*

6. If John is older than Mary and Mary is younger than Jane, then 6.____

   A. twice Mary's age is less than the sum of the ages of John and Jane
   B. the sum of the ages of John and Mary exceeds the age of Jane
   C. the ages of John and Jane are equal
   D. three times Mary's age equals the sum of the ages of John and Jane

7. John is older than Mary, Henry is older than Mary. 7.____
   It follows, therefore, that

   A. John and Henry are the same age
   B. the sum of the ages of John and Mary exceeds the age of Henry
   C. Mary's age is less than half of the sum of John's and Henry's ages
   D. none of the preceding three statements is true

8. The average of 9 numbers is 70. 8.____
   It follows that

   A. the sum of the numbers is 630
   B. the median of the numbers is 70
   C. the median of the numbers cannot be 70
   D. no two of the numbers can be equal

9. John is twice as old as Mary. 9.____
   The only statement about their ages which is NOT true is

   A. in five years, John will be twice as old as Mary
   B. in five years, the sum of their ages will be 10 more than the present sum of their ages
   C. Mary's present age is one-third of the sum of their present ages
   D. two years ago, the difference between their ages was the same as it will be two years hence

10. A is taller than B; C is 2 inches shorter than B. 10.____
    The one statement of the following four statements which is NOT necessarily true is

    A. B is taller than C
    B. A is taller than C
    C. A is taller than C by more than 2 inches
    D. B's height is the average of the heights of A and C

KEY (CORRECT ANSWERS)

1.	A	6.	A
2.	B	7.	C
3.	C	8.	D
4.	C	9.	A
5.	B	10.	D

TEST 3

DIRECTIONS: Each question or incomplete statement is followed by several suggested answers or completions. Select the one that BEST answers the question or completes the statement. *PRINT THE LETTER OF THE CORRECT ANSWER IN THE SPACE AT THE RIGHT.*

1. A stenographer can BEST deal with the situation which arises when her pencil breaks during dictation by 1.____

   A. asking the person dictating to lend her one
   B. being equipped at every dictation with several pencils
   C. going back to her desk to secure another one
   D. making a call to the supply room for some pencils

2. Accuracy is of greater importance than speed in filing CHIEFLY because 2.____

   A. city offices have a tremendous amount of filing to do
   B. fast workers are usually inferior workers
   C. there is considerable difficulty in locating materials which have been filed incorrectly
   D. there are many varieties of filing systems which may be used

3. Many persons dictate so rapidly that they pay little attention to matters of punctuation and English, but they expect their stenographers to correct errors. 3.____
   This statement implies MOST clearly that stenographers should be

   A. able to write acceptable original reports when required
   B. good citizens as well as good stenographers
   C. efficient clerks as well as good stenographers
   D. efficient in language usage

4. A typed letter should resemble a picture properly framed. 4.____
   This statement MOST emphasizes

   A. accuracy B. speed
   C. convenience D. neatness

5. Of the following, the CHIEF advantage of the use of a mechanical check is that it 5.____

   A. guards against tearing in handling the check
   B. decreases the possibility of alteration in the amount of the check
   C. tends to prevent the mislaying and loss of checks
   D. facilitates keeping checks in proper order for mailing

6. Of the following, the CHIEF advantage of the use of a dictating machine is that the 6.____

   A. stenographer must be able to take rapid dictation
   B. person dictating tends to make few errors
   C. dictator may be dictating letters while the stenographer is busy at some other task
   D. usual noise in an office is lessened

7. The CHIEF value of indicating enclosures beneath the identification marks on the lower left side of a letter is that it 7.____

   A. acts as a check upon the contents before mailing and upon receiving a letter
   B. helps determine the weight for mailing
   C. is useful in checking the accuracy of typed matter
   D. requires an efficient mailing clerk

8. The one of the following which is NOT an advantage of the window envelope is that it 8.____

   A. saves time since the inside address serves also as an outside address
   B. gives protection to the address from wear and tear of the mails
   C. lessens the possibility of mistakes since the address is written only once
   D. tends to be much easier to seal than the plain envelope

9. A question as to proper syllabication of a word at the end of a line may BEST be settled by consulting 9.____

   A. the person who dictated the letter
   B. a shorthand manual
   C. a dictionary
   D. a file of letters

10. Mailing a letter which contains many erasures is undesirable CHIEFLY because 10.____

   A. paper should not be wasted
   B. some stenographers are able to carry on some of the correspondence in an office without consulting their superiors
   C. correspondence should be neat
   D. erasures indicate that the dictator was not certain of what he intended to say in the letter

---

KEY (CORRECT ANSWERS)

1.	B	6.	C
2.	C	7.	A
3.	D	8.	D
4.	D	9.	C
5.	B	10.	C

TEST 4

DIRECTIONS: Each question or incomplete statement is followed by several suggested answers or completions. Select the one that BEST answers the question or completes the statement. *PRINT THE LETTER OF THE CORRECT ANSWER IN THE SPACE AT THE RIGHT.*

1. A charter operates for a city in somewhat the same fashion as 1.____

   A. the United States Supreme Court functions with regard to federal legislation
   B. the United States Constitution operates for the entire country
   C. the Governor functions for New York State
   D. a lease for a landlord

2. All civil employees should be especially interested in the activities of the United States Supreme Court PRIMARILY because 2.____

   A. its decisions provide certain kinds of important general rules
   B. the Supreme Court consists of nine persons appointed by the President
   C. the American Constitution is the finest document which man has ever produced
   D. the President's plan for reorganization of the court may be revived

3. Of the following, it is most frequently argued that labor problems are of concern to the civil employee PRIMARILY because 3.____

   A. the problems of labor are the same as the problems of government
   B. newspapers carry considerable information about labor problems
   C. the civil employee is a wage or salary earner
   D. a government is of the people, for the people, and by the people

4. Warfare in any part of the world should be of interest to the civil employee PRIMARILY as a result of the fact that 4.____

   A. strict American neutrality is secured by not permitting the sale of munitions to any country at war
   B. war has not been declared though warfare is raging
   C. the United States participates in the meetings of the UN
   D. facilities for transportation and communication have produced a "smaller" world

5. Cities regulate certain aspects of housing CHIEFLY because 5.____

   A. the city is the largest municipality in the country
   B. zoning is the concern of all residents of the city
   C. housing affects health
   D. the state constitution makes regulation optional

6. In general, it is PROBABLY true that the functions which a city administers are those 6.____

   A. most necessary to the preservation of the well-being of its residents
   B. of little or no interest to private business
   C. forbidden to the state
   D. not capable of being financed by private business

7. There is no more convincing mark of a cultured speaker or writer than accuracy of statement. 7.____
This statement stresses the importance of

A. new ideas
B. facts
C. acquiring a pleasing speaking voice
D. poise

8. When a department is called, the voice which answers the telephone is, to the person calling, the department itself. 8.____
This statement implies *most clearly* that

A. only one person should answer the telephone in each office
B. a clerk with a pleasing, courteous telephone manner is an asset to an office
C. an efficient clerk will terminate all telephone conversations as quickly as possible
D. making personal telephone calls is looked upon with disfavor in some offices

9. Probably the CHIEF advantage of filling higher vacancies by promotion is that this procedure 9.____

A. stimulates the worker to improve his work and general knowledge and technique
B. provides an easy check on the work of the individual
C. eliminates personnel problems in a department
D. harmonizes the work of one department with that of all other departments

10. Greatest efficiency is reached when filing method and filing clerk are harmoniously adjusted to the needs of an office. 10.____
This statement means *most nearly* that

A. the filing method is more important than the clerk in securing the successful handling of valuable papers
B. almost any clerk can do office filing well
C. a good clerk using a good filing system assures good filing
D. every office needs a filing system

KEY (CORRECT ANSWERS)

1.	B	6.	A
2.	A	7.	B
3.	C	8.	B
4.	D	9.	A
5.	C	10.	C

TEST 5

DIRECTIONS: Each question or incomplete statement is followed by several suggested answers or completions. Select the one that BEST answers the question or completes the statement. *PRINT THE LETTER OF THE CORRECT ANSWER IN THE SPACE AT THE RIGHT.*

1. Your superior, Mr. Hotchkiss, is in conference and has requested that he not be disturbed. 1.____
   The condition under which you would MOST probably disturb the conference is:

   A. A Mr. Smith, whom you have not seen before, says he has important business with Mr, Hotchkiss
   B. Mrs. Hotchkiss telephones, saying there has been a serious accident at home
   C. You do not know how a certain letter should be filed and wish to ask the advice of Mr. Hotchkiss
   D. A fellow clerk wishes to ask Mr. Hotchkiss whether a particular city department handles certain matters

2. Your superior directs you to find certain papers. You know the purpose for which the papers are to be used. In the course of your search for the papers, you come across certain material which would be very useful for the purpose to be served by the papers. 2.____
   You should

   A. bring the papers to your superior and ask whether he wants the other materials
   B. go to your superior immediately and ask whether he wishes both the materials and the papers or only one of the two
   C. bring to your superior the other materials, together with the papers you were directed to find
   D. bring only the other materials to your superior and point out the manner in which these materials are of greater value than the papers

3. If a fellow employee asks you a question to which you do not know the answer, you should say, 3.____

   A. "I don't know. What's the difference?"
   B. "The answer to that question forms no part of my duties here."
   C. "My dear sir, the thing for you to do is to look the matter up yourself because it is your responsibility, not mine."
   D. "I'm sorry. I don't know."

4. In general, it is PROBABLY true that MOST people are 4.____

   A. so self-seeking that they pay no attention to the wants, needs, or behavior of others
   B. so changeable that one never knows what his fellow employee is likely to do next
   C. not worth the trouble to bother about
   D. quite ready to help others

5. Of the following, the one which is NOT a reason for avoiding clerical errors is that 5.____

   A. time is lost
   B. money is wasted
   C. many clerks are very intelligent
   D. serious consequences may follow

6. Of the following, the MAIN reason for keeping a careful record of incoming mail is that 6.___

   A. some people are less industrious than others
   B. this record helps to speed up outgoing mail
   C. this record is a kind of legal evidence
   D. this information may be useful in answering questions which may arise

7. Of the following, the MAIN reason for using a calculating machine is that 7.___

   A. a lesser knowledge of arithmetic is needed
   B. a more attractive product is obtained
   C. greater speed and accuracy are obtained
   D. it is not difficult to learn how to operate a calculating machine

8. Of the following, the MAIN reason for being polite over the telephone is that 8.___

   A. persons who are speaking over the telephone cannot see each other
   B. politeness makes for pleasant business relationships
   C. it is not at all difficult or costly to be courteous
   D. one's voice is of great importance because voice reflects mood

9. Because telephone directories contain printed pages, they are called books. This statement assumes *most nearly* that 9.___

   A. some books do not contain printed pages
   B. not all telephone directories are books which contain printed pages
   C. material which contains printed pages is called a book
   D. all books which contain printed pages are called telephone directories

10. Mr. Cross must be using a budget because he has been able to reduce his unnecessary expenses. 10.___
    On the basis of only the material included in this statement, it may MOST accurately be said that this statement assumes that

   A. all people who use budgets lower certain types of expenses
   B. some people who do not use budgets reduce unnecessary expenses
   C. some people who use budgets do not reduce unnecessary expenses
   D. all types of expenses are reduced by the use of a budget

---

KEY (CORRECT ANSWERS)

1.	B	6.	D
2.	C	7.	C
3.	D	8.	B
4.	D	9.	C
5.	C	10.	A

EXAMINATION SECTION
TEST 1

DIRECTIONS: Each question or incomplete statement is followed by several suggested answers or completions. Select the one that BEST answers the question or completes the statement. *PRINT THE LETTER OF THE CORRECT ANSWER IN THE SPACE AT THE RIGHT.*

Questions 1-50.

DIRECTIONS: Select the letter of the word or phrase which means the SAME or NEARLY THE SAME as the capitalized word.

1. DISCURSIVE 1.____
   A. desultory B. eclectic
   C. meretricious D. fragmentary

2. NOISOME 2.____
   A. hostile B. noisily C. secretive D. noxious

3. HEGEMONY 3.____
   A. wealth B. flight C. jewels D. leadership

4. BEREFT 4.____
   A. depraved B. diseased C. deprived D. deranged

5. BRUIT 5.____
   A. bully B. threat C. rumor D. award

6. ALBESCENT 6.____
   A. whitish B. fictitious
   C. forgiving D. bluish

7. PERQUISITE 7.____
   A. requirements B. gift
   C. rubescence D. progeny

8. AGNOMEN 8.____
   A. first name B. middle name
   C. surname D. nickname

9. PERMUTE 9.____
   A. alter B. extol C. condone D. rip apart

10. IMPECCANT 10.____
    A. blameless B. faulty
    C. dishonest D. contingent

11. DISSOLUTE 11.____

A. honorable
B. profligate
C. fortuitous
D. flexible

12. PERSPICUITY 12.____

A. punctuality
B. plumosity
C. lucidity
D. affluency

13. OBTUND 13.____

A. make less acute
B. encircle
C. obturate
D. make more rotund

14. LONGANIMITY 14.____

A. linear measure
B. envy
C. forbearance
D. geriatrics

15. GAINSAY 15.____

A. profit B. reward C. concoct D. deny

16. MAGNILOQUENT 16.____

A. cathartic
B. wealthy
C. bombastic
D. supercilious

17. FRUCTUOUS 17.____

A. acerbic
B. productive
C. hostile
D. argumentative

18. IMPOLITIC 18.____

A. injudicious
B. unrealistic
C. impious
D. improvident

19. SCREED 19.____

A. ridicule B. harangue C. select D. foment

20. VAINGLORY 20.____

A. loyalty
B. patriotism
C. obstinacy
D. pride

21. TUMEFY 21.____

A. sweeten B. soften C. swell D. hate

22. DICHOTOMY 22.____

A. plan B. echelon C. diathesis D. division

23. EDACIOUS 23.____

A. untruthful
B. voracious
C. fortuitous
D. bombastic

24. NECROLOGY 24.____

A. obituary B. marriage register
C. birth list D. alien list

25. HEBETUDE 25.____

A. hostility B. lethargy
C. spontaneity D. futility

26. PERNICKETY 26.____

A. talkative B. fastidious
C. perturbing D. ludicrous

27. RAILLERY 27.____

A. freightage B. depot
C. banter D. innuendo

28. DESUETUDE 28.____

A. disgust B. disbelief
C. disuse D. displeasure

29. RECIDIVIST 29.____

A. factotum B. repeater C. barrister D. sibling

30. CORUSCATE 30.____

A. sparkle B. dullish C. encircle D. rescue

31. DIDACTIC 31.____

A. spiteful B. acerbic
C. moody D. instructive

32. PORTENTOUS 32.____

A. fragile B. ominous C. erudite D. sagacious

33. FRACTIOUS 33.____

A. split B. broken C. unruly D. diffident

34. ENDEMIC 34.____

A. extraneous B. indigenous
C. mollescent D. confluent

35. CONCINNITY 35.____

A. elegance B. circle C. diaconal D. exponiable

36. FUSCOUS 36.____

A. dusky B. illegitimate
C. flashily D. tortuous

37. PUNCHINELLO 37.____

A. savant B. lecturer C. pundit D. clown

38. MISCREANT 38.____

A. injudicious
B. misogynous
C. villainous
D. rapacious

39. HABILIMENT 39.____

A. penitentiary
B. garment
C. litigation
D. slander

40. PROLOCUTOR 40.____

A. spokesman
B. barrister
C. savant
D. pundit

41. REDOUBTABLE 41.____

A. questionable
B. bearable
C. formidable
D. hopeful

42. DECREMENT 42.____

A. profit B. stipend C. loss D. annuity

43. VORTICAL 43.____

A. rushing B. jumping C. flying D. whirling

44. VIATOR 44.____

A. traveler
B. philosopher
C. apothecary
D. magician

45. GERMANE 45.____

A. unrelated B. turbid C. turgid D. relevant

46. TRANSPONIABLE 46.____

A. propitious
B. prosaic
C. transposable
D. egregious

47. SPOLIATE 47.____

A. worsen B. despoil C. upbraid D. debilitate

48. SEBIFEROUS 48.____

A. sebaceous
B. castigating
C. relenting
D. contumacious

49. SUCCOR 49.____

A. collect B. aid C. contrive D. consort

50. TERGIVERSATION 50.____

A. loyalty B. constancy C. apostasy D. hypocrisy

KEY (CORRECT ANSWERS)

1.	A	11.	B	21.	C	31.	D	41.	C
2.	D	12.	C	22.	D	32.	B	42.	C
3.	D	13.	A	23.	B	33.	C	43.	D
4.	C	14.	C	24.	A	34.	B	44.	A
5.	C	15.	D	25.	B	35.	A	45.	D
6.	A	16.	C	26.	B	36.	A	46.	C
7.	B	17.	B	27.	C	37.	D	47.	B
8.	D	18.	A	28.	C	38.	C	48.	A
9.	A	19.	B	29.	B	39.	B	49.	B
10.	A	20.	D	30.	A	40.	A	50.	C

TEST 2

Questions 1-25.

DIRECTIONS: Select the letter of the word or phrase which means the OPPOSITE or NEARLY THE OPPOSITE as the capitalized word.

1. EMEND 1.____

A. alleviate B. worsen C. conserve D. spend

2. HIBERNAL 2.____

A. hopeful B. spiteful C. hateful D. summery

3. OBSEQUIOUS 3.____

A. independent B. pernicious
C. contrite D. conserving

4. CAPRICIOUS 4.____

A. unsteady B. predictable
C. relentless D. irretrievable

5. INSENSATE 5.____

A. intelligent B. articulate
C. animate D. untiring

6. LUGUBRIOUS 6.____

A. displeased B. doleful
C. petulant D. happy

7. PUERILE 7.____

A. untainted B. affluent C. mature D. facetious

8. EXCULPATORY 8.____

A. blameworthy B. faultless
C. spotless D. tireless

9. DISTRAIT 9.____

A. talkative B. cooperative
C. festive D. attentive

10. APPOSITE 10.____

A. irrelevant B. distasteful
C. honorable D. flighty

11. CONTUMACIOUS 11.____

A. dishonorable B. disregardful
C. punctual D. obedient

12. CACOPHONY 12.____

A. harmony B. musical C. penurious D. absolute

13. DILATORY 13.____
A. delaying B. lethargic C. prompt D. voracious

14. QUONDAM 14.____
A. skillful
B. previous
C. propitiative
D. present

15. AMORPHOUS 15.____
A. definite
B. herculean
C. powerful
D. worthless

16. BANAL 16.____
A. contrite
B. resourceful
C. unusual
D. diffident

17. PROLIX 17.____
A. erroneous
B. hypocritical
C. terse
D. egregious

18. INTREPID 18.____
A. cowardly
B. niggardly
C. noisily
D. timidly

19. ANTITHESIS 19.____
A. nadir
B. similarity
C. corollary
D. magnetic

20. MORIBUND 20.____
A. resolute
B. living
C. incongruous
D. decrepit

21. LOQUACITY 21.____
A. silence
B. garrulity
C. thoughtfulness
D. hyperbole

22. ANTEDILUVIAN 22.____
A. picturesque
B. oily
C. modern
D. watery

23. PLAINTIVE 23.____
A. mournful B. restful C. farcical D. joyful

24. BUCOLIC 24.____
A. rural B. urban C. odorous D. tiresome

25. CONTROVERT 25.____

A. argue B. consort C. agree D. displease

Questions 26-50.

DIRECTIONS: Select the MISSPELLED word in each group.

26. A. siege B. wierd C. seize D. cemetery 26.____

27. A. equaled B. bigoted C. benefited D. kaleideoscope 27.____

28. A. blamable B. bullrush C. questionnaire D. irascible 28.____

29. A. tobagganed B. acquiline C. capillary D. cretonne 29.____

30. A. daguerrotype B. elegiacal C. iridescent D. inchoate 30.____

31. A. bayonet B. braggadocio C. corollary D. connoiseur 31.____

32. A. equinoctial B. fusillade C. fricassee D. potpouri 32.____

33. A. octameter B. impressario C. hyetology D. hieroglyphics 33.____

34. A. innanity B. idyllic C. fylfot D. inimical 34.____

35. A. liquefy B. rarefy C. putrify D. sapphire 35.____

36. A. canonical B. stupified C. millennium D. memorabilia 36.____

37. A. paraphenalia B. odyssey C. onomatopoeia D. osseous 37.____

38. A. peregrinate B. pecadillo C. reptilian D. uxorious 38.____

39. A. Pharisaical B. vicissitude C. puissance D. wainright 39.____

40. A. holocaust B. tesselate C. scintilla D. staccato 40.____

41. A. surveillance B. trousseau C. suzeranity D. trekked 41.____

42. A. sexagenarian B. solioquy C. versimilitude D. laity 42.____

43. A. semophore B. ubiquitous C. insouciant D. homiletic 43.____

44. A. tatterdemalion B. terrestrial 44.____
C. gladiolus D. infinitestimal

45. A. tranquility B. enrolment 45.____
C. eleemosynary D. plebescite

46. A. battalion B. vilify 46.____
C. fusilage D. inoculate

47. A. boundries B. fuchsia 47.____
C. plaguy D. cotillion

48. A. hinderance B. obbligato 48.____
C. dumbfound D. picnicking

49. A. sacrilegious B. sibylline 49.____
C. sergeant D. temperment

50. A. vermilion B. paraffin 50.____
C. floculent D. violoncello

KEY (CORRECT ANSWERS)

1. B	11. D	21. A	31. D	41. C
2. D	12. A	22. C	32. D	42. C
3. A	13. C	23. D	33. B	43. A
4. B	14. D	24. B	34. A	44. D
5. C	15. A	25. C	35. C	45. D
6. D	16. C	26. B	36. B	46. C
7. C	17. C	27. D	37. A	47. A
8. A	18. A	28. B	38. B	48. A
9. D	19. B	29. B	39. D	49. D
10. A	20. B	30. A	40. B	50. C

CORRECT SPELLING

26. weird
27. kaleidoscope
28. bulrush
29. aquiline
30. daguerreotype
31. connoisseur
32. potpourri
33. impresario
34. inanity
35. putrefy
36. stupefied
37. paraphernalia
38. peccadillo
39. wainwright
40. tessellate
41. suzerainty
42. verisimilitude
43. semaphore
44. infinitesimal
45. plebiscite
46. fuselage
47. boundaries
48. hindrance
49. temperament
50. flocculent

TEST 3

DIRECTIONS: Each question or incomplete statement is followed by several suggested answers or completions. Select the one that BEST answers the question or completes the statement. *PRINT THE LETTER OF THE CORRECT ANSWER IN THE SPACE AT THE RIGHT.*

Questions 1-25.

DIRECTIONS: Select the MISSPELLED word in each group.

1. A. pimentoes B. desperadoes C. innuendoes D. mementoes 1.____

2. A. miscellaneous B. vignette C. arhythmic D. vicessitude 2.____

3. A. exorcise B. plagiarize C. macadamise D. mortise 3.____

4. A. spiritural B. capriccio C. beriberi D. doggerel 4.____

5. A. acreage B. annoint C. counterfeit D. eighths 5.____

6. A. cameos B. sopranos C. mottoes D. dynamoes 6.____

7. A. aquarium B. acqueduct C. balustrade D. bivouacked 7.____

8. A. chrysanthemum B. frolicsome C. guage D. idiosyncrasy 8.____

9. A. isosceles B. inundate C. mimicked D. minerology 9.____

10. A. beneficent B. pastime C. phthisis D. pavillion 10.____

11. A. pusillanimity B. repetition C. scythe D. spermacetti 11.____

12. A. variegated B. coolly C. corrolary D. commissariat 12.____

13. A. doggerel B. evenness C. gossamer D. gossippy 13.____

14. A. hemorrhage B. japanned C. bachanal D. supersede 14.____

15. A. ballbriggan B. barrette C. annihilate D. ammeter 15.____

16. A. cinnabar B. epiglotis 16.____

C. cachinnate D. chaparral

17. A. philipic B. flagellate 17.____
C. medallion D. obligate

18. A. questionnaire B. whipoorwill 18.____
C. ukulele D. jinrikisha

19. A. dishabille B. naphtha 19.____
C. placque D. diapason

20. A. rhinoceros B. hippopotamus 20.____
C. dinossaur D. giraffe

21. A. inditement B. hierarchy 21.____
C. hawser D. monogomous

22. A. timbre B. tremulo 22.____
C. nicknack D. cybernetics

23. A. zuchinni B. familiar 23.____
C. similar D. frontispiece

24. A. homolagous B. homogonous 24.____
C. homunculous D. pabulum

25. A. withheld B. gutteral C. dumbbell D. glutinous 25.____

Questions 26-60.

DIRECTIONS: In each of the following groups of sentences, one sentence is INCORRECT because it includes an error in grammar, usage, sentence structure, or punctuation. Indicate the INCORRECT sentence in each group.

26. A. I do not say exactly that these stories are true; I only say that I do not believe them. 26.____
B. My old fountain pen, which never leaked or clogged, is broken and I can use it no further.
C. Compare the quality of our papers with any other papers in the same price range. There is just no comparison.
D. Today's news, in the words of a famous Frenchman, is in yesterday's newspaper; tomorrow's, in today's.

27. A. She objected to his reading comics and told him to put it away. 27.____
B. The patient said that the doctor had ordered him to lie down every day after dinner for two hours and that he had, in fact, lain down for more than three hours.
C. We are likely to run out of money before our vacation is over, and we shall have to borrow some from our friends.
D. We are confident that you will appoint whomever is best suited for the position.

28. A. "Age is like love: it cannot be hit." - Thomas Dekker 28.____
B. The question Mary refused to answer was: "did you see Mr. Clark actually leave the building?
C. This information, namely, that we are going out of business, is accurate.
D. The Joneses' house is in excellent condition because Mr. and Mrs. Jones take such good care of it.

29. A. He, not she, is the one to go because he is better prepared than her; thus he can do the job as well as she and we can be sure that it will be done properly. 29.____
B. She had no sooner entered the office and begun to type than the bell announced the first coffee break of the day.
C. While there has been considerable scholarly interest in the subject, there have been hardly any scientific experiments of any value in the field.
D. I played the song "Getting to Know You" from the record "The King and I."

30. A. Take one of these books which are to be discarded because it has no value any more. 30.____
B. Although the period has lasted for more than thirty minutes, the students are not tired and can do much more work.
C. Williams has a most unique idea for the school play, and he plans to discuss it with his teacher.
D. After cleaning the house, my mother lay in the hammock for an hour; then she went shopping.

31. A. Sunrise High School, with an enrollment of 1,200 boys and 1,100 girls, is the largest in the state. 31.____
B. I was pleased with his visiting me in the hospital as I was lonely and depressed at the time.
C. To type with your feet spread out in all directions is considered to be an example of poor typewriting technique.
D. First-class furs like first-class diamonds are very expensive; both the initial cost and the year-to-year upkeep require a great deal of money.

32. A. Not having received a reply to my letter of June 8, I am writing again to ask if anything is wrong. 32.____
B. She asked, "Whom does Mr. Jones feel should have won the typewriting medal?"
C. Strawberries and cream is a perfect summer dessert, and I have asked my mother to serve the dish frequently.
D. Either Mary or the boys have broken the window, and I mean to find out immediately before they do further damage.

33. A. Of the ladies present at the meeting, three were chosen to be delegates to the annual convention to be held the following May. 33.____
B. The reason I succeeded is that I prepared thoroughly for the test.
C. I heard her say that the window was broken by the ball and damaged the vase in the living room.
D. They have been chosen for two reasons – namely, because they are intelligent and because they are conscientious.

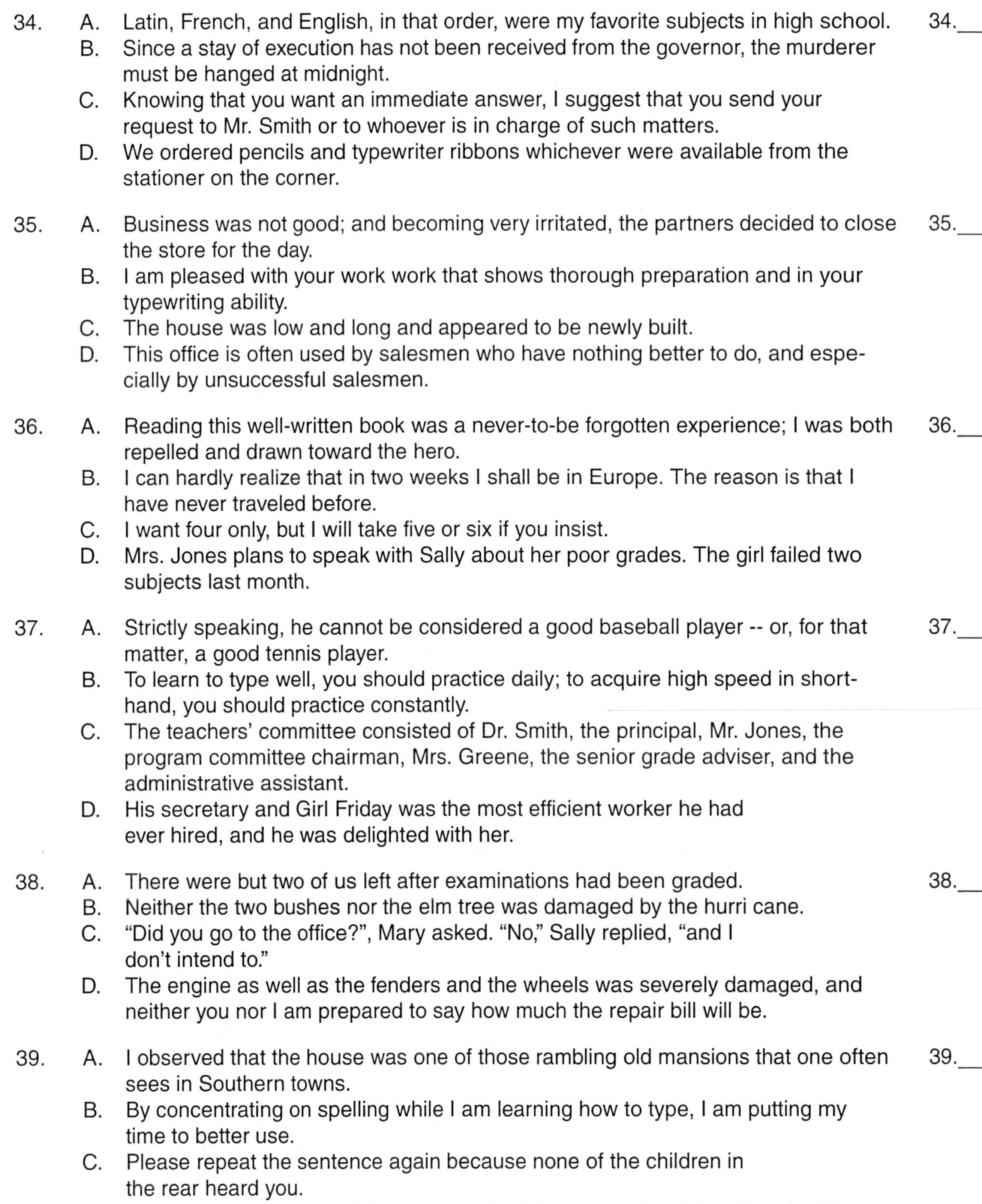

34. A. Latin, French, and English, in that order, were my favorite subjects in high school. 34.____
B. Since a stay of execution has not been received from the governor, the murderer must be hanged at midnight.
C. Knowing that you want an immediate answer, I suggest that you send your request to Mr. Smith or to whoever is in charge of such matters.
D. We ordered pencils and typewriter ribbons whichever were available from the stationer on the corner.

35. A. Business was not good; and becoming very irritated, the partners decided to close the store for the day. 35.____
B. I am pleased with your work work that shows thorough preparation and in your typewriting ability.
C. The house was low and long and appeared to be newly built.
D. This office is often used by salesmen who have nothing better to do, and especially by unsuccessful salesmen.

36. A. Reading this well-written book was a never-to-be forgotten experience; I was both repelled and drawn toward the hero. 36.____
B. I can hardly realize that in two weeks I shall be in Europe. The reason is that I have never traveled before.
C. I want four only, but I will take five or six if you insist.
D. Mrs. Jones plans to speak with Sally about her poor grades. The girl failed two subjects last month.

37. A. Strictly speaking, he cannot be considered a good baseball player -- or, for that matter, a good tennis player. 37.____
B. To learn to type well, you should practice daily; to acquire high speed in shorthand, you should practice constantly.
C. The teachers' committee consisted of Dr. Smith, the principal, Mr. Jones, the program committee chairman, Mrs. Greene, the senior grade adviser, and the administrative assistant.
D. His secretary and Girl Friday was the most efficient worker he had ever hired, and he was delighted with her.

38. A. There were but two of us left after examinations had been graded. 38.____
B. Neither the two bushes nor the elm tree was damaged by the hurri cane.
C. "Did you go to the office?", Mary asked. "No," Sally replied, "and I don't intend to."
D. The engine as well as the fenders and the wheels was severely damaged, and neither you nor I am prepared to say how much the repair bill will be.

39. A. I observed that the house was one of those rambling old mansions that one often sees in Southern towns. 39.____
B. By concentrating on spelling while I am learning how to type, I am putting my time to better use.
C. Please repeat the sentence again because none of the children in the rear heard you.
D. The police have arrested three men: John Winters, 27, Brooklyn; Timothy Flynn, 26, Brooklyn; and Sheldon Young, 26, Queens.

40. A. "I have laid the book down," she said. "I shall now go to sleep." 40.____
B. The policeman, not the gangsters, merits our approval despite the fact that crime is made to be so attractive on television.
C. "Did you finish your composition yet?" Sally asked. "No," Jane replied.
D. Where can I find out who wrote, "What you don't know would make a great book"?

41. A. I read in a book that boys and girls today are taller and heavier than their parents were at the same age. How interesting! 41.____
B. John said that from where he was sitting in the ball park, he could hardly see the batter and the pitcher.
C. He expects to be graduated from Morningside High School in January instead of June as he has been taking extra summer courses.
D. Speaking of employment, have many new jobs been created on Long Island as a result of all the industries which have settled there during the past five years?

42. A. I have risen at five o'clock in the morning for the past twenty years, and I am still in excellent physical condition. 42.____
B. I have laid the letter on my employer's desk several times, but he still has not signed it.
C. We felt that if he would have tried harder, he might have passed the examination.
D. I am angry with John principally because I am angry at the comments he made at the rally last night.

43. A. I met a friend of father's the other day in Boland and Ryan's suburban store. 43.____
B. Less men were hurt this year than last because of the intensive safety precautions which have been introduced.
C. During several months -- that is, June, July, and August -- school is closed.
D. We need all types of skills in our office -- for example, stenographers, typists, IBM operators, duplicator operators, and typist-clerks.

44. A. The paper says that civil liberties is the principaltopic of conversation in Washington today. 44.____
B. I do not know why -- but perhaps I shouldn't try to find out at this time.
C. I would have preferred to do nothing until he came, so I decided to lie down.
D. As I was entering the office, I heard a bell clang right behind me, which gave me a bad fright.

45. A. As I went deeper and deeper into the forest, the light became dimmer and dimmer. 45.____
B. Did he actually say, "I can't do a thing for you"? I can imagine him being so ungrateful.
C. After he had seen the play OKLAHOMA (which he had been told in advance was excellent), he decided to to to the theater much more often.
D. Bill Carlton did not go to college, which shocked his family and astonished his friends because Bill was a really good student.

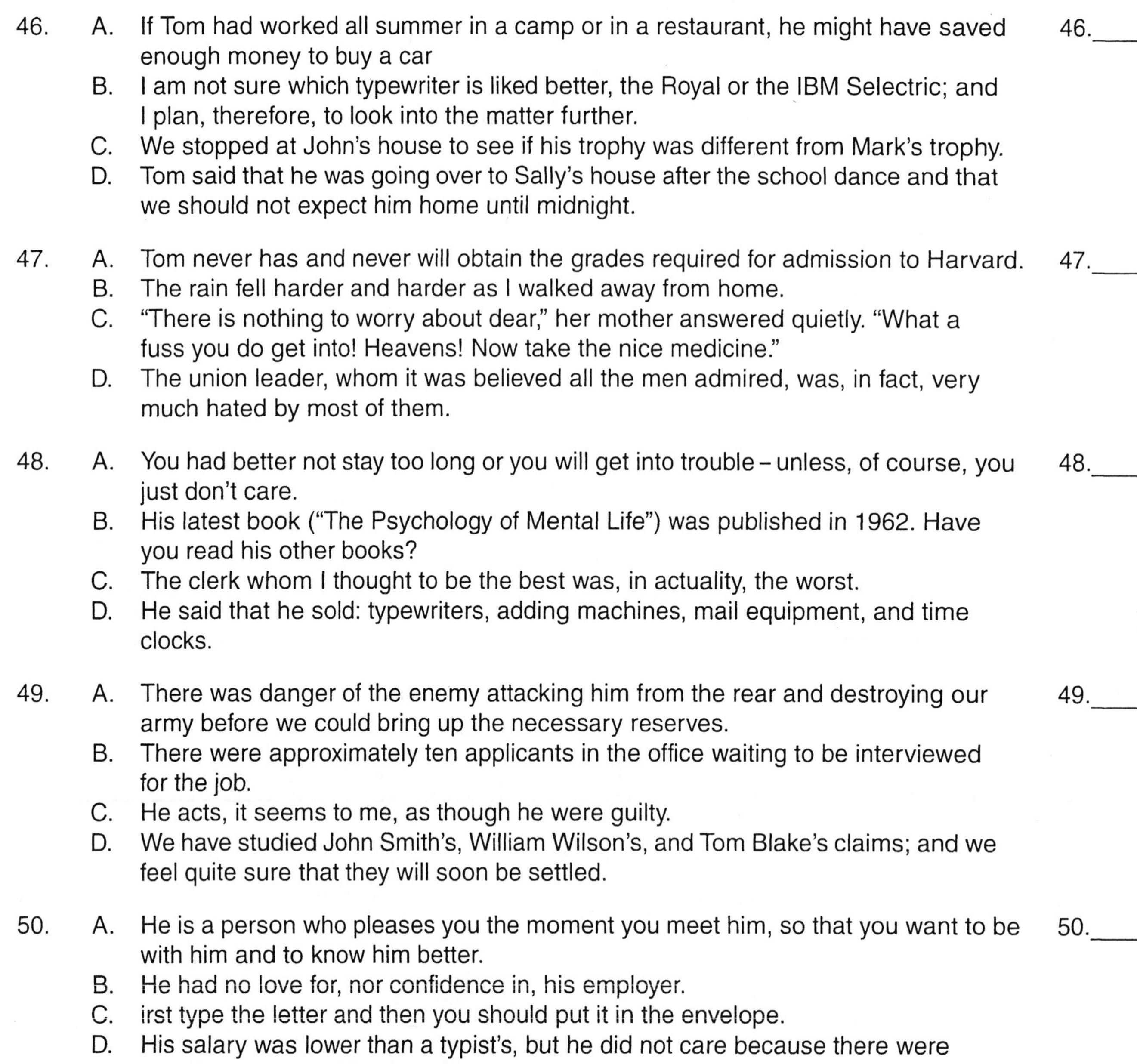

46. A. If Tom had worked all summer in a camp or in a restaurant, he might have saved enough money to buy a car 46.____
    B. I am not sure which typewriter is liked better, the Royal or the IBM Selectric; and I plan, therefore, to look into the matter further.
    C. We stopped at John's house to see if his trophy was different from Mark's trophy.
    D. Tom said that he was going over to Sally's house after the school dance and that we should not expect him home until midnight.

47. A. Tom never has and never will obtain the grades required for admission to Harvard. 47.____
    B. The rain fell harder and harder as I walked away from home.
    C. "There is nothing to worry about dear," her mother answered quietly. "What a fuss you do get into! Heavens! Now take the nice medicine."
    D. The union leader, whom it was believed all the men admired, was, in fact, very much hated by most of them.

48. A. You had better not stay too long or you will get into trouble – unless, of course, you just don't care. 48.____
    B. His latest book ("The Psychology of Mental Life") was published in 1962. Have you read his other books?
    C. The clerk whom I thought to be the best was, in actuality, the worst.
    D. He said that he sold: typewriters, adding machines, mail equipment, and time clocks.

49. A. There was danger of the enemy attacking him from the rear and destroying our army before we could bring up the necessary reserves. 49.____
    B. There were approximately ten applicants in the office waiting to be interviewed for the job.
    C. He acts, it seems to me, as though he were guilty.
    D. We have studied John Smith's, William Wilson's, and Tom Blake's claims; and we feel quite sure that they will soon be settled.

50. A. He is a person who pleases you the moment you meet him, so that you want to be with him and to know him better. 50.____
    B. He had no love for, nor confidence in, his employer.
    C. irst type the letter and then you should put it in the envelope.
    D. His salary was lower than a typist's, but he did not care because there were excellent opportunities for advancement.

KEY (CORRECT ANSWERS)

1.	A	11.	D	21.	D	31.	D	41.	B
2.	D	12.	C	22.	B	32.	B	42.	C
3.	C	13.	D	23.	A	33.	C	43.	B
4.	A	14.	C	24.	A	34.	D	44.	D
5.	B	15.	A	25.	B	35.	B	45.	B
6.	D	16.	B	26.	C	36.	A	46.	D
7.	B	17.	A	27.	D	37.	C	47.	A
8.	C	18.	B	28.	B	38.	C	48.	D
9.	D	19.	C	29.	A	39.	C	49.	A
10.	D	20.	C	30.	C	40.	C	50.	C

CORRECT SPELLING

1. pimentos or pimientos
2. vicissitude
3. macadamize
4. spiritual
5. anoint
6. dynamos
7. aqueduct
8. gauge
9. mineralogy
10. pavilion
11. spermaceti
12. corollary
13. gossipy
14. bacchanal
15. balbriggan
16. epiglottis
17. philippic
18. whippoorwill
19. plaque
20. dinosaur
21. monogamous
22. tremolo
23. zucchini
24. homologous
25. guttural

TEST 4

DIRECTIONS: Each question or incomplete statement is followed by several suggested answers or completions. Select the one that BEST answers the question or completes the statement. *PRINT THE LETTER OF THE CORRECT ANSWER IN THE SPACE AT THE RIGHT.*

Questions 1-10.

DIRECTIONS: In each of the following groups of sentences, one sentence is INCORRECT because it includes an error in grammar, usage, sentence structure, or punctuation. Indicate the INCORRECT sentence in each group.

1. A. I typed this letter you may not believe this, but it is true in four minutes. 1.____
   B. "It is clear (the message read) that the Muscle Shoals development is but a small part of the potential public usefulness of the entire Tennessee River." - D.E. Lilienthal
   C. Shaw made his first plunge into controversy: he rose to his feet, shaking with nerves and heard himself speaking.
   D. After the reading of the will, he opened up the strong box and divided up the money among the relatives present.

2. A. "It is one of those cars that go faster than 90 miles an hour," said the salesman. 2.____
   B. Elementary school children are not the only ones who are tardy; it is also true of high school and college students.
   C. My handsome (?) brother who is in college writes that he is "having a wonderful time"; he is, however, not doing too well scholastically.
   D. A number of clerks were drinking coffee during the coffee break; the number of cups they drank was unbelievable.

3. A. He asked what had caused the accident. She replied that she did not know since she had not been present when it had occurred. 3.____
   B. The new party headed by Prime Minister Wilson advocated government for the people, not by the people.
   C. Five hundred yards of cloth are sufficient to do the work satisfactorily, and I plan to work continually until I finish.
   D. She thought it would be all right for her to do the work in advance of the due date owing to the fact that none of the machines was being used by others.

4. A. "Oh! please stop that," he said; but when he looked up, they were nowhere to be seen. 4.____
   B. The president of the company often told us workers of his experiences as a penniless, untrained beginner forty years ago.
   C. The family showed its approval of the plan and decided to leave for Detroit, Michigan, on May 18th, or, if delay was unavoidable, on May 25th.
   D. "I'm not buying," he said, "it's too expensive."

5. A. We expect in the next decade to more than hold our own in our race to the moon. 5.____
   B. The teachers who have been considering the annual promotion plan today gave their report to the principal.
   C. You are likely to find him sitting beside the brook in the park.
   D. I shall have eaten by the time we go if my plans proceed according to schedule.

6. A. If you must know -- of course, however, this is a secret -- Billy just asked to borrow my car. 6.____
   B. The job is over with, and neither my wife nor my children will ever persuade me to do it again.
   C. You ought not to have said what you said, and I suggest that you apologize at once.
   D. His friends had begun to understand how much he had done for the organization, but then they seemed to forget everything.

7. A. Unlike Bill and me, Ted looks really good in a stylish suit. 7.____
   B. They have good teachers in our high schools; therefore, I plan to become a high school teacher.
   C. Do you remember the name of the book? the author? the copyright date? the name of the publisher? of the editor?
   D. The secretary and treasurer of the firm intends to hold a meeting with his president within a week or two.

8. A. Foreign films may be interesting, but I do not see them often. I usually prefer listening to music. 8.____
   B. Court reporting has always fascinated me, but last spring I went to a lecture by a famous reporter. Then I made up my mind to be a reporter.
   C. Haven't I asked you a hundred times to take the damaged typewriter to the repair shop which is in the store next to Jones's Candy Store?
   D. Your typewriter should be kept absolutely clean and should be dusted as soon as you have completed your day's work.

9. A. The salesmen felt very pleased when they heard the manager say that their sales for the month of July, August, and September were much higher than that for the same months the previous year. 9.____
   B. Four hundred dollars is too much to pay for these typewriters; I therefore suggest that you do some additional shopping before you make a final decision.
   C. John said that he had swum around the lake three times and that he was now eligible for his swimming certificate.
   D. I recently read "Trade Winds" in <u>The Saturday Review.</u>

10. A. Neither being sufficiently prepared for it, both brothers had to apply for additional training at the technical school. 10.____
B. The question was laid before them, and after weeks of argument it was still unsettled.
C. If all goes satisfactorily -- and why shouldn't it? --we shall be in Europe before the middle of May.
D. In his first year he was only an office boy, and in his fifth year he was president of the company.

Questions 11-40.

DIRECTIONS: In each of the following groups, three abbreviations are correct and one abbreviation is INCORRECT. Select the INCORRECT abbreviation.

11. A. ampere - ampe. B. against all risks - a.a.r. 11.____
C. absent - ab. D. abridged - abr.

12. A. author's correction - ac 12.____
B. Alaska - Ala.
C. to the end - ad fin.
D. to infinity - ad inf.

13. A. at the place - ad loc. B. address - ads. 13.____
C. advertisement - advt. D. of age - o.a.

14. A. agency - agy. B. agreement - agt. 14.____
C. also known as - a.k.a. D. anonymous - anony.

15. A. approximate - ap. B. appendix - appdx. 15.____
C. application - appl. D. aqueous - aq.

16. A. Arkansas - Ark. B. article - art. 16.____
C. assumed - assmd. D. assignment - asgmt.

17. A. assortment - astmt. B. Association - Assn. 17.____
C. Assistant - Asst. D. Attorney - Atty.

18. A. avoirdupois - av. B. barometer - bmtr. 18.____
C. bundle - bdl. D. boulevard - Bl.

19. A. bill of sale - B/S B. bought - bt. 19.____
C. book value - b.v. D. carat - ct.

20. A. California - Calif. B. Canadian - Canadn. 20.____
C. Congress - C. D. calendar - cal.

21. A. century - centy. B. carbon copy - c.c. 21.____
C. catalogue - cat. D. Cashier - Cash.

22. A. centigram - eg B. at buyer's risk - c.e. 22.____
C. chemical - ch. D. chapter - C

23. A. circumference - circum. B. chart - cht. 23.____
C. chronological - chron. D. circuit - ckt.

24. A. Connecticut - Conn. 24.____
B. Corresponding Secretary - Corr. Sec.
C. commercial - cml.
D. carloa.d - cl.

25. A. coupon - cpn. 25.____
B. center-to-center - c-c
C. currency - curr.
D. cylinder - cyl.

26. A. called - dit
B. delivered - dlvd. 26.____
C. decibel - db
D. debenture - deb.

27. A. pennyweight - dwt. 27.____
B. destination - dstn.
C. end of month payment - e.o.m.p.
D. day - dy.

28. A. for example - e.g.
B. entered - entd. 28.____
C. and wife - et vir
D. executive - ex.

29. A. foolscap - fcsp.
B. and the following - f. 29.____
C. export - exp.
D. examples - exx.

30. A. first-in, first-out - fifo 30.____
B. fluid - fid.
C. forward - fwd.
D. freight - frt.

31. A. great gross - gr. gr.
B. General Agent - GA 31.____
C. gills - gi.
D. government - govt.

32. A. freight on board - f.o.b. 32.____
B. guaranteed - gtd.
C. hardware - hdw.
D. hogshead - hhd.

33. A. Headquarters - Hqtrs.
B. general - gn. 33.____
C. the same - id.
D. that is - i.e.

34. A. unknown - incog.
B. information - info 34.____
C. the limit - in lim.
D. the same as - i.q.

35. A. Japan - Jap.
B. Justices - JJ 35.____
C. junction - junct.
D. large - la.

36. A. in the place cited - cit. loc. 36.____
B. large - lge.
C. last-in, first-out - lifo
D. lines - ll.

37. A. machinery - mach.
B. place of the seal - L.S. 37.____
C. merchandise - mdse.
D. memorandum - memo.

38. A. no account - N/A
B. mortgage - mtge. 38.____

C. manufactured - mfd   D. miscellaneous - misc.

39. A. note well - n.b.   B. unanimous - nem. con.   39.____
C. it is not clear - n.l.l.   D. name unknown - n.u.

40. A. on account - o/a   B. out of print - o.p.   40.____
C. obsolete - obs.   D. equal parts - pa. e.

41. A. premium - pm.   B. promissory note - pr. n.   41.____
C. temporarily - pro tem.   D. quality - qly.

42. A. resolution - res.   B. which see - q.v.   42.____
C. received - recd.   D. so stated - scil.

43. A. the following - seq.   B. signature - sign.   43.____
C. security - sec.   D. signed - /S/

44. A. sold - sld.   B. seller's option - s.o.   44.____
C. without issue - s. pr.   D. syllable - syl.

45. A. sections - ss.   B. let it stand - stet.   45.____
C. standard - std.   D. storage - stge.

46. A. trial balance - T.B.   B. Territory - Terr.   46.____
C. till forbidden - t.f.   D. tablespoon - tbsp.

47. A. Treasurer - Treas.   B. title page - t.p.   47.____
C. next month - ult.   D. tax - tx.

48. A. as directed - ut dic.   B. versus - v.   48.____
C. as above - u.s.   D. see below - i.v.

49. A. vice versa - v.v.   B. write - vid.   49.____
C. warrant - wt.   D. namely - viz.

50. A. waybill - WB   B. wharfage - whge.   50.____
C. without rights - w.r.   D. various - var.

KEY (CORRECT ANSWERS)

1.	D	11.	A	21.	A	31.	A	41.	B
2.	B	12.	B	22.	D	32.	A	42.	D
3.	B	13.	D	23.	A	33.	A	43.	B
4.	D	14.	D	24.	B	34.	C	44.	C
5.	D	15.	B	25.	C	35.	C	45.	D
6.	B	16.	C	26.	B	36.	A	46.	B
7.	B	17.	A	27.	C	37.	D	47.	C
8.	B	18.	B	28.	C	38.	B	48.	D
9.	A	19.	D	29.	A	39.	C	49.	B
10.	A	20.	B	30.	B	40.	D	50.	C

TEST 5

Questions 1-25.

DIRECTIONS: In each of the following groups, one pronunciation is incorrect. Indicate the letter which corresponds to the INCORRECT pronunciation. Listed below each word is the pronunciation. The accented syllable is indicated by capital letters.

1. A. buttress - BUT ris 1.____
   B. cabal - ke BAL
   C. cardiography - kar di OG re fi
   D. comparator - kom PAR e tr

2. A. decoy (N) - DE coy 2.____
   B. homogeneity - ho me je NE i ti
   C. frigate - FRIG it
   D. mimosa - mi mo SA

3. A. irrefragable - i REF re ge bl 3.____
   B. atavist - AT e vist
   C. apian - a PIAN
   D. irrevocable - i REV e ke bl

4. A. apothem - a POTH m 4.____
   B. foulard - foo LARD
   C. despicable - DES pik a bl
   D. empathy - EM pe thi

5. A. demesne - di MAN 5.____
   B. cardiogram - KARD i o gram
   C. detonate - DET e nat
   D. equitable - EK wi te bl

6. A. desultory - de SUL to ri 6.____
   B. dyspepsia - dis PEP si e
   C. errantry - ER ent ri
   D. ersatz - er ZATS

7. A. equipage - e KWIP ij 7.____
   B. petrous - PET res
   C. empennage - EM pi nij
   D. erubescent - er oo BES ent

8. A. pejorative - pe JER a tiv 8.____
   B. sequestrator - SE kwes tra tor
   C. seraph - SER ef
   D. speciosity - spe shi OS e ti

9. A. appanage - AP e nij 9.____
B. imprimatur - im PRIM a ter
C. grimace - gri MAS
D. hospitable - HOS pi te bl

10. A. irascible - i RAS e bl 10.____
B. inextricable - in EKS tri ke bl
C. ignominy - ig NOM i ni
D. inexorable - in EK ser a bl

11. A. lucubrate - LU kyoo brat 11.____
B. confrere - KON frar
C. congeries - kon JER ez
D. erythemic - e RE the mik

12. A. recognizable - re keg NIZ a bl 12.____
B. reverberate - re VUR be rat
C. exigency - EX se jen si
D. chimerical - ke MER i kl

13. A. interpolate - in TUR pe lat 13.____
B. combatant - kom BAT ant
C. formidable - FOR mi de bl
D. recoup - ri KOOP

14. A. interstice - IN tur stis 14.____
B. indecorous - in DEK e res
C. contuse - ken TOOZ
D. incomparable - in KOM per e bl

15. A. fastigiate - FAS tij i at 15.____
B. interregnum - in ter REG nem
C. gondola - GON de le
D. artisan - AR te zn

16. A. municipal - mu NIC e pl 16.____
B. lamentable - la MEN te bl
C. mischievous - MIS chi ves
D. positively - POS e tiv le

17. A. necromancy - nek re MAN si 17.____
B. artificer - ar TIF e ser
C. pyramidal - pi RAM e dl
D. miscreate - mis kri AT

18. A. homeopathy - ho mi OP e thi 18.____
B. exculpate - EKS kel pat
C. panoply - pan e PLI
D. homicidal - hom e SID l

19. A. aspirant - e SPIR ent 19.____
    B. vehicular - ve HIK yoo ler
    C. admirable - AD me re bl
    D. impious - im PI es

20. A. apotheosis - e poth i O sis 20.____
    B. deciduous - di SIJ oo es
    C. fragmentary - frag MEN ta ri
    D. infamous - IN fe mes

21. A. inquiry - in KWIR i 21.____
    B. irate - I rat
    C. eczema - EK se me
    D. irreparable - ir re PAR a bl

22. A. finance (N) - fe NANS 22.____
    B. jocose - jo KOS
    C. exacerbate - ig ZAS er bat
    D. assiduity - a SID yoo i ti

23. A. arroyo - e ROI o 23.____
    B. dissonant - DIS e nent
    C. badinage - BAD n ij
    D. aboretum - ar BE re tum

24. A. ambuscade - am BUS kad 24.____
    B. brougham - BROO em
    C. banality - be NAL i ti
    D. chimerical - ki MER i kl

25. A. stalactite - ste LAK tit 25.____
    B. amplify - am pli FI
    C. talipot - TAL i pot
    D. tamale - te MA li

Questions 26-50.

DIRECTIONS: In each of the following groups, one word is syllabicated incorrectly. Select the word in each group that is INCORRECTLY syllabicated.

26. A. frag il i ty B. jet ti son 26.____
    C. ka ty did D. lar ghet to

27. A. in eluct able B. lap i dar y 27.____
    C. mac ro cosm D. no tice a bly

28. A. join er y B. no tar i al 28.____
    C. in ex tirp able D. nov el ette

29. A. o le og ra phy B. frang i bil i ty 29.____
    C. ped es tal D. pe tu ni a

30. A. pet ti ness B. sac red 30.____
C. in fam ous D. saf flow er

31. A. scraw ny B. sep a ra tist 31.____
C. scratch es D. inter mit tent

32. A. se ques ter B. scour ge 32.____
C. shin er D. shift y

33. A. tal is man B. ten e brif ic 33.____
C. sep tu a gen ar i an D. tem po rize

34. A. tongu ing B. u nis o nal 34.____
C. tend en tious D. se rag lio

35. A. voy a geur B. shim mer 35.____
C. too tle D. tra peze

36. A. wash a ble B. vo tress 36.____
C. yeo man ry D. he rit a ble

37. A. her e sy B. i con o clast 37.____
C. ib ex D. in do lent

38. A. i so stat ic B. herb a ceous 38.____
C. is let D. lan dau

39. A. iam bic B. la nig er ous 39.____
C. me ringue D. mort ga gee

40. A. lang uor B. mo les ta tion 40.____
C. O hi o an D. rev e nue

41. A. pe dic u lar B. re lin quish 41.____
C. pan dem ic D. pam phle teer

42. A. rel e van cy B. psy chom o tor 42.____
C. mon e ti za tion D. a gron o my

43. A. pej o ra tion B. pe dun cle 43.____
C. a nach ro nous D. a non y mous

44. A. ap ro pos B. prun el la 44.____
C. psal ter y D. ca nas ta

45. A. ban dit ti B. pru ri ent 45.____
C. ban ana D. can non ry

46. A. chat ti ly B. cho ler ic 46.____
C. con tu me li ous D. dolt ish

47. A. ee ri ly B. don zel 47.____
C. ed i tor i al D. ex tra or di nar y

48. A. flat ter y B. ex u vi al 48.____
C. flax y D. hi jack er

49. A. Hi ma la yas B. i dly 49.____
C. ex ul tan cy D. i de a

50. A. jin go is tic B. id i o syn era sy 50.____
C. in ter pel late D. mil ler

KEY (CORRECT ANSWERS)

1.	D	11.	D	21.	D	31.	D	41.	D
2.	D	12.	A	22.	D	32.	B	42.	B
3.	C	13.	B	23.	D	33.	C	43.	A
4.	A	14.	A	24.	A	34.	C	44.	B
5.	B	15.	A	25.	B	35.	A	45.	C
6.	A	16.	B	26.	A	36.	D	46.	B
7.	A	17.	A	27.	A	37.	C	47.	C
8.	A	18.	C	28.	C	38.	B	48.	B
9.	B	19.	D	29.	B	39.	A	49.	C
10.	C	20.	C	30.	C	40.	A	50.	D

CLERICAL ABILITIES TEST

Clerical aptitude involves the ability to perceive pertinent detail in verbal or tabular material, to observe differences in copy, to proofread words and numbers, and to avoid perceptual errors in arithmetic computation.

NATURE OF THE TEST

Four types of clerical aptitude questions are presented in the Clerical Abilities Test. There are 120 questions with a short time limit. The test contains 30 questions on name and number checking, 30 on the arrangement of names in correct alphabetical order, 30 on simple arithmetic, and 30 on inspecting groups of letters and numbers. The questions have been arranged in groups or cycles of five questions of each type. The Clerical Abilities Test is primarily a test of speed in carrying out relatively simple clerical tasks. While accuracy on these tasks is important and will be taken into account in the scoring, experience has shown that many persons are so concerned about accuracy that they do the test more slowly than they should. Competitors should be cautioned that speed as well as accuracy is important to achieve a good score.

HOW THE TEST IS ADMINISTERED

Each competitor should be given a copy of the test booklet with sample questions on the cover page, an answer sheet, and a medium No. 2 pencil. Ten minutes are allowed to study the directions and sample questions and to answer the questions in the proper boxes on the two pages.

The separate answer sheet should be used for the test proper. Fifteen minutes are allowed for the test.

HOW THE TEST IS SCORED

The correct answers should be counted and recorded. The number of incorrect answers must also be counted because one-fourth of the number of incorrect answers is subtracted from the number of right answers. An omission is considered as neither a right nor a wrong answer. The score on this test is the number of right answers minus one-fourth of the number of wrong answers (fractions of one-half or less are dropped). For example, if an applicant had answered 89 questions correctly and 10 questions incorrectly, and had omitted 1 question, his score would be 87.

EXAMINATION SECTION

DIRECTIONS: This test contains four kinds of questions. There are some of each kind on each page in the booklet. The time limit for the test will be announced by the examiner.

Use the special pencil furnished by the examiner in marking your answers on the separate answer sheet. For each question, there are five suggested answers. Decide which answer is correct, find the number of the question on the answer sheet, and make a *solid black mark* between the dotted lines just below the letter of your answer. If you wish to change your answer, erase the first mark completelydo not merely cross it out.

SAMPLE QUESTIONS

In each line across the page there are three names or numbers that are much alike. Compare the three names or numbers and decide which ones are exactly alike. On the Sample Answer Sheet at the right, mark the answer-

A if ALL THREE names or numbers are exactly ALIKE
B if only the FIRST and SECOND names or numbers are exactly ALIKE
C if only the FIRST and THIRD names or numbers are exactly ALIKE
D if only the SECOND and THIRD names or numbers are exactly ALIKE
E if ALL THREE names or numbers are DIFFERENT

I.	Davis Hazen	David Hozen	David Hazen
II.	Lois Appel	Lois Appel	Lois Apfel
III.	June Allan	Jane Allan	Jane Allan
IV.	10235	10235	10235
V.	32614	32164	32614

It will be to your advantage to learn what A, B, C, D, and E stand for. If you finish the sample questions before you are told to turn to the test, study them.

SAMPLE ANSWER SHEET

	A	B	C	D	E
I					
II					
III					
IV					
V					
VI					
VII					

In the next group of sample questions, there is a name in a box at the left, and four other names in alphabetical order at the right. Find the correct space for the boxed name so that it will be in alphabetical order with the others, and mark the letter of that space as your answer.

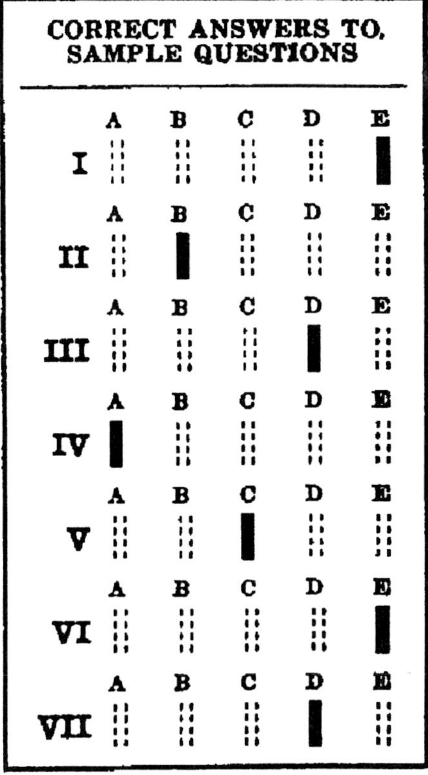

CORRECT ANSWERS TO SAMPLE QUESTIONS

	A	B	C	D	E
I					▮
II		▮			
III				▮	
IV	▮				
V			▮		
VI					▮
VII				▮	

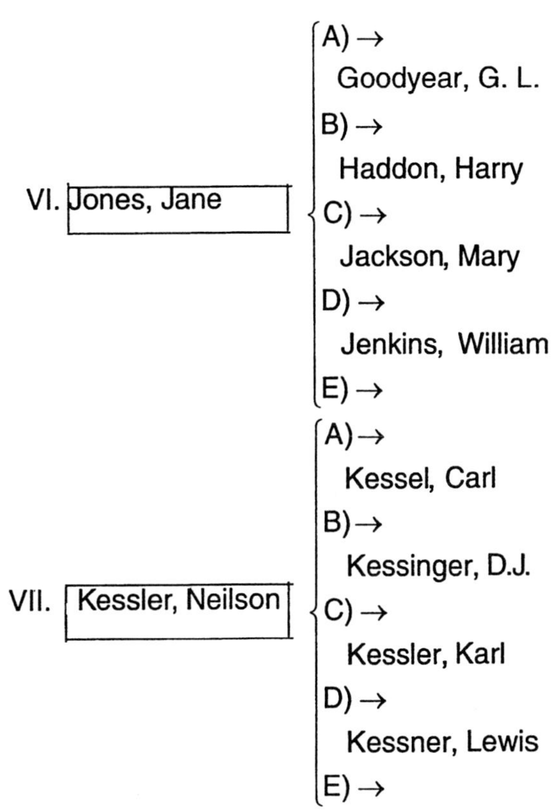

VI. Jones, Jane

A) →
Goodyear, G. L.
B) →
Haddon, Harry
C) →
Jackson, Mary
D) →
Jenkins, William
E) →

VII. Kessler, Neilson

A) →
Kessel, Carl
B) →
Kessinger, D.J.
C) →
Kessler, Karl
D) →
Kessner, Lewis
E) →

DIRECTIONS: In the following questions, complete the equation and find your answer among the list of suggested answers. Mark the Sample Answer Sheet A, B, C or D for the answer you obtained; or if your answer is not among these, mark E for that question.

VIII. Add:

$$\begin{array}{r} 22 \\ +\ 33 \\ \hline \end{array}$$

A) 44 B) 45
C) 54 D) 55
E) none of these

IX. Subtract:

$$\begin{array}{r} 24 \\ -\ \ 3 \\ \hline \end{array}$$

A) 20 B) 21
C) 27 D) 29
E) none of these

X. Multiply:

$$\begin{array}{r} 25 \\ \times\ \ 5 \\ \hline \end{array}$$

A) 100 B) 115
C) 125 D) 135
E) none of these

XI. Divide:

$6 \overline{)126}$

A) 20 B) 22
C) 24 D) 26
E) none of these

Directions: There is one set of suggested answers for the next group of sample questions. Do not try to memorize these answers, because there will be a different set on each page in the test.

To find the answer to a question, find which suggested answer contains numbers and letters all of which appear in the question. If no suggested answer fits, mark E for that question.

XII. 8NK9GT46
XIII. T97Z6L3K
XIV. Z7GK398N
XV. 3K946GZL
XVI. ZN738KT9

Suggested Answers
- A = 7,9,G,K
- B = 8,9,T,Z
- C = 6,7,K,Z
- D = 6,8,G,T
- E = none of these

SAMPLE ANSWER SHEET

	A	B	C	D	E
VIII					
IX					
X					
XI					
XII					
XIII					
XIV					
XV					
XVI					

CORRECT ANSWERS TO SAMPLE QUESTIONS

	A	B	C	D	E
VIII				■	
IX		■			
X			■		
XI					■
XII				■	
XIII			■		
XIV	■				
XV					■
XVI		■			

After you have marked your answers to all the questions on the Sample Answer Sheets on this page and on the front page of the booklet, check them with the answers in the boxes marked Correct Answers to Sample Questions.

In questions 1 through 5, compare the three names or numbers, and mark

- A if ALL THREE names or numbers are exactly ALIKE
- B if only the FIRST and SECOND names or numbers are exactly ALIKE
- C if only the FIRST and THIRD names or numbers are exactly ALIKE
- D if only the SECOND and THIRD names or numbers are exactly ALIKE
- E if ALL THREE names or numbers are DIFFERENT

1.	5261383	5261383	5261338
2.	8125690	8126690	8125609
3.	W. E. Johnston	W. E. Johnson	W. E. Johnson
4.	Vergil L. Muller	Vergil L. Muller	Vergil L. Muller
5.	Atherton R. Warde	Asheton R. Warde	Atherton P. Warde

In questions 6 through 10, find the correct place for the name in the box.

6. Hackett, Gerald

- A) →
- Habert, James
- B) →
- Hachett, J. J.
- C) →
- Hachetts, K, Larson
- D) →
- Hachettson, Leroy
- E) →

7. Margenroth, Alvin

- A) →
- Margeroth, Albert
- B) →
- Margestein, Dan
- C) →
- Margestein, David
- D) →
- Margue, Edgar
- E) →

8. Bobbitt, Olivier E.

- A) →
- Bobbitt, D. Olivier
- B) →
- Bobbitt, Olive B.
- C) →
- Bobbitt, Olivia H.
- D) →
- Bobbitt, R. Olivia
- E) →

9. Mosely, Werner

- A) →
- Mosely, Albert J.
- B) →
- Mosley, Alvin
- C) →
- Mosley, S. M.
- D) →
- Mozley, Vinson N.
- E) →

10. Youmuns, Frank L.

- A) →
- Youmons, Frank G.
- B) →
- Youmons, Frank H.
- C) →
- Youmons, Frank K.
- D) →
- Youmons, Frank M.
- E) →

GO ON TO THE NEXT COLUMN.

Answers

11. Add:
$$\begin{array}{r} 4\ 3 \\ +\ 3\ 2 \\ \hline \end{array}$$
A) 55 B) 65 C) 66 D) 75 E) none of these

12. Subtract:
$$\begin{array}{r} 8\ 3 \\ -\ \ \ 4 \\ \hline \end{array}$$
A) 73 B) 79 C) 80 D) 89 E) none of these

13. Multiply:
$$\begin{array}{r} 4\ 1 \\ \times\ \ \ 7 \\ \hline \end{array}$$
A) 281 B) 287 C) 291 D) 297 E) none of these

14. Divide:
$6 \overline{)\,3\ 0\ 6}$
A) 44 B) 51 C) 52 D) 60 E) none of these

15. Add:
$$\begin{array}{r} 3\ 7 \\ +\ 1\ 5 \\ \hline \end{array}$$
A) 42 B) 52 C) 53 D) 62 E) none of these

For each question below, find which one of the suggested answers appears in that question.

16. 6 2 5 K 4 P T G

17. L 4 7 2 T 6 V K

18. 3 5 4 L 9 V T G

19. G 4 K 7 L 3 5 Z

20. 4 K 2 9 N 5 T G

Suggested Answers
- A=4, 5, K, T
- B=4, 7, G, K
- C=2, 5, G, L
- D=2, 7, L, T
- E=none of these

GO ON TO THE NEXT PAGE.

In questions 21 through 25, compare the three names or numbers, and mark the answer

A if ALL THREE names or numbers are exactly ALIKE
B if only the FIRST and SECOND names or numbers are exactly ALIKE
C if only the FIRST and THIRD names or numbers are exactly ALIKE
D if only the SECOND and THIRD names or numbers are exactly ALIKE
E if ALL THREE names or numbers are DIFFERENT

21.	2395890	2395890	2395890
22.	1926341	1926347	1926314
23.	E. Owens McVey	E. Owen McVey	E. Owen McVay
24.	Emily Neal Rouse	Emily Neal Rowse	Emily Neal Rowse
25.	H. Merritt Audubon	H. Merriott Audubon	H. Merritt Audubon

In questions 26 through 30, find the correct place for the name in the box.

26. Watters, N. O.
A) →
Waters, Charles L.
B) →
Waterson, Nina P.
C) →
Watson, Nora J.
D) →
Wattwood, Paul A.
E) →

27. Johnston, Edward
A) →
Johnston, Edgar R.
B) →
Johnston, Edmond
C) →
Johnston, Edmund
D) →
Johnstone, Edmund A.
E) →

28. Rensch, Adeline
A) →
Ramsay, Amos
B) →
Remschel, Augusta
C) →
Renshaw, Austin
D) →
Rentzel, Becky
E) →

29. Schnyder, Maurice
A) →
Schneider, Martin
B) →
Schneider, Mertens
C) →
Schnyder, Newman
D) →
Schreibner, Norman
E) →

30. Freedenburg, C. Erma
A) →
Freedenberg, Emerson
B) →
Freedenberg, Erma
C) →
Freedenberg, Erma E.
D) →
Freedinberg, Erma F.
E) →

GO ON TO THE NEXT COLUMN.

Answers

31. Subtract: $68 - 47$
A) 10 B) 11 C) 20 D) 22 E) none of these

32. Multiply: 50×8
A) 400 B) 408 C) 450 D) 458 E) none of these

33. Divide: $9 \overline{)180}$
A) 20 B) 29 C) 30 D) 39 E) none of these

34. Add: $78 + 63$
A) 131 B) 140 C) 141 D) 151 E) none of these

35. Subtract: $89 - 70$
A) 9 B) 18 C) 19 D) 29 E) none of these

For each question below, find which one of the suggested answers appears in that question.

36. 9 G Z 3 L 4 6 N

37. L 5 N K 4 3 9 V

38. 8 2 V P 9 L Z 5

39. V P 9 Z 5 L 8 7

40. 5 T 8 N 2 9 V L

Suggested Answers
A=4, 9, L, V
B=4, 5, N, Z
C=5, 8, L, Z
D=8, 9, N, V
E=none of these

GO ON TO THE NEXT PAGE.

In questions 41 through 45, compare the three names or numbers, and mark the answer
A if ALL THREE names or numbers are exactly ALIKE
B if only the FIRST and SECOND names or numbers are exactly ALIKE
C if only the FIRST and THIRD names or numbers are exactly ALIKE
D if only the SECOND and THIRD names or numbers are exactly ALIKE
E if ALL THREE names or numbers are DIFFERENT

41.	6219354	6219354	6219354
42.	2312793	2312793	2312793
43.	1065407	1065407	1065047
44.	Francis Ransdell	Frances Ramsdell	Francis Ramsdell
45.	Cornelius Detwiler	Cornelius Detwiler	Cornelius Detwiler

In questions 46 through 50, find the correct place for the name in the box.

46. **DeMattia, Jessica**
A) →
DeLong, Jesse
B) →
DeMatteo, Jessie
C) →
Derby, Jessie S.
D) →
DeShazo, L. M.
E) →

47. **Theriault, Louis**
A) →
Therien, Annette
B) →
Therien, Elaine
C) →
Thibeault, Gerald
D) →
Thiebeault, Pierre
E) →

48. **Gaston, M. Hubert**
A) →
Gaston, Dorothy M.
B) →
Gaston, Henry N.
C) →
Gaston, Isabel
D) →
Gaston, M. Melvin
E) →

49. **SanMiguel, Carlos**
A) →
SanLuis, Juana
B) →
Santilli, Laura
C) →
Stinnett, Nellie
D) →
Stoddard, Victor
E) →

50. **DeLaTour, Hall F.**
A) →
Delargy, Harold
B) →
DeLathouder, Hilda
C) →
Lathrop, Hillary
D) →
LaTour, Hulbert E.
E) →

GO ON TO THE NEXT COLUMN.

Answers

51. Multiply: 62×5 — A) 300 B) 310 C) 315 D) 360 E) none of these

52. Divide: $3 \overline{)153}$ — A) 41 B) 43 C) 51 D) 53 E) none of these

53. Add: $47 + 21$ — A) 58 B) 59 C) 67 D) 68 E) none of these

54. Subtract: $87 - 42$ — A) 34 B) 35 C) 44 D) 45 E) none of these

55. Multiply: 37×3 — A) 91 B) 101 C) 104 D) 114 E) none of these

For each question below, find which one of the suggested answers appears in that question.

56. N 5 4 7 T K 3 Z

57. 8 5 3 V L 2 Z N

58. 7 2 5 N 9 K L V

59. 9 8 L 2 5 Z K V

60. Z 6 5 V 9 3 P N

Suggested Answers:
A=3, 8, K, N
B=5, 8, N, V
C=3, 9, V, Z
D=5, 9, K, Z
E=none of these

GO ON TO THE NEXT PAGE.

In questions 61 through 65, compare the three names or numbers, and mark the answer

- A if ALL THREE names or numbers are exactly ALIKE
- B if only the FIRST and SECOND names or numbers are exactly ALIKE
- C if only the FIRST and THIRD names or numbers are exactly ALIKE
- D if only the SECOND and THIRD names or numbers are exactly ALIKE
- E if ALL THREE names or numbers are DIFFERENT

61.	6452054	6452654	6452054
62.	8501268	8501268	8501286
63.	Ella Burk Newham	Ella Burk Newnham	Elena Burk Newnham
64.	Jno. K. Ravencroft	Jno. H. Ravencroft	Jno. H. Ravencoft
65.	Martin Wills Pullen	Martin Wills Pulen	Martin Wills Pullen

In questions **66** through 70, find the correct place for the name in the box.

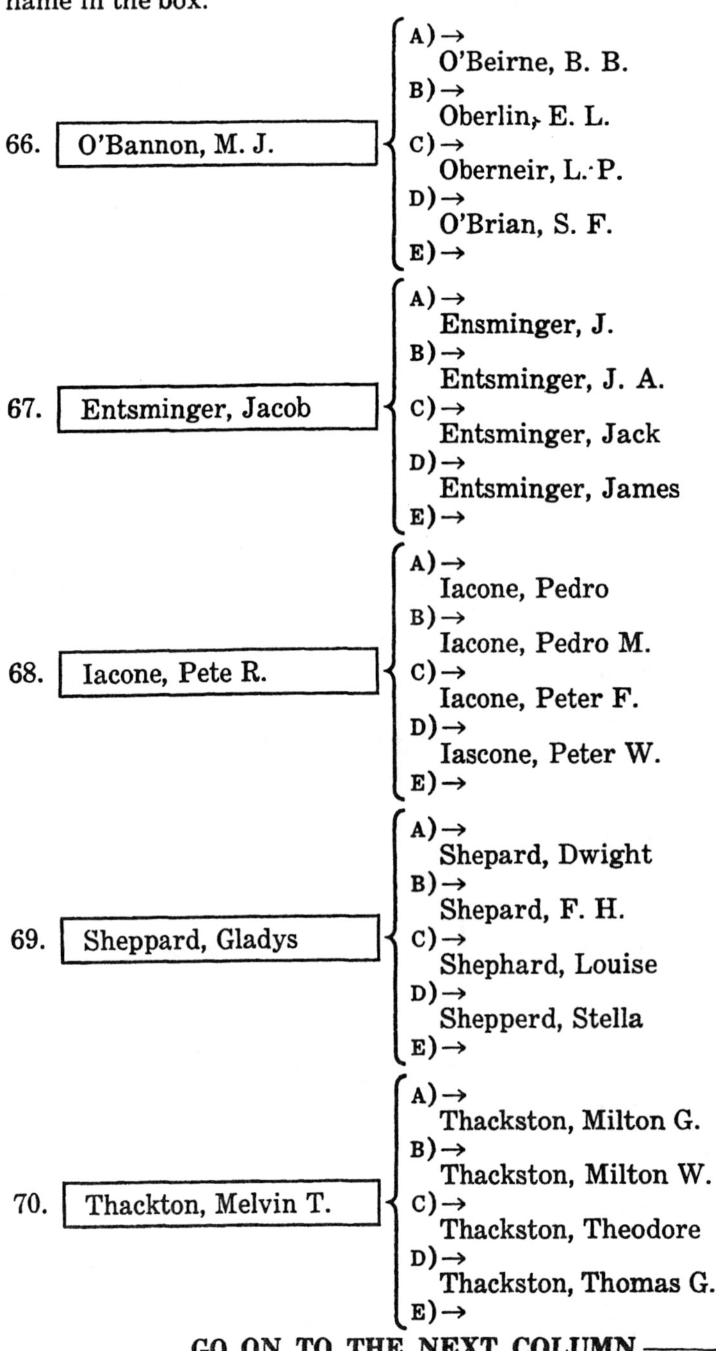

66. O'Bannon, M. J.
- A) →
- O'Beirne, B. B.
- B) →
- Oberlin, E. L.
- C) →
- Oberneir, L. P.
- D) →
- O'Brian, S. F.
- E) →

67. Entsminger, Jacob
- A) →
- Ensminger, J.
- B) →
- Entsminger, J. A.
- C) →
- Entsminger, Jack
- D) →
- Entsminger, James
- E) →

68. Iacone, Pete R.
- A) →
- Iacone, Pedro
- B) →
- Iacone, Pedro M.
- C) →
- Iacone, Peter F.
- D) →
- Iascone, Peter W.
- E) →

69. Sheppard, Gladys
- A) →
- Shepard, Dwight
- B) →
- Shepard, F. H.
- C) →
- Shephard, Louise
- D) →
- Shepperd, Stella
- E) →

70. Thackton, Melvin T.
- A) →
- Thackston, Milton G.
- B) →
- Thackston, Milton W.
- C) →
- Thackston, Theodore
- D) →
- Thackston, Thomas G.
- E) →

GO ON TO THE NEXT COLUMN. →

Answers

71. Divide: $7 \overline{)\,3\ 5\ 7}$ — A) 51 B) 52 C) 53 D) 54 E) none of these

72. Add: $58 + 27$ — A) 75 B) 84 C) 85 D) 95 E) none of these

73. Subtract: $86 - 57$ — A) 18 B) 29 C) 38 D) 39 E) none of these

74. Multiply: 68×4 — A) 242 B) 264 C) 272 D) 274 E) none of these

75. Divide: $9 \overline{)\,6\ 3\ 9}$ — A) 71 B) 73 C) 81 D) 83 E) none of these

For each question below, find which one of the suggested answers appears in that question.

76. 6 Z T N 8 7 4 V

77. V 7 8 6 N 5 P L

78. N 7 P V 8 4 2 L

79. 7 8 G 4 3 V L T

80. 4 8 G 2 T N 6 L

Suggested Answers
- A = 2, 7, L, N
- B = 2, 8, T, V
- C = 6, 8, L, T
- D = 6, 7, N, V
- E = none of these

GO ON TO THE NEXT PAGE.

In questions 81 through 85, compare the three names or numbers, and mark the answer

- A if ALL THREE names or numbers are exactly ALIKE
- B if only the FIRST and SECOND names or numbers are exactly ALIKE
- C if only the FIRST and THIRD names or numbers are exactly ALIKE
- D if only the SECOND and THIRD names or numbers are exactly ALIKE
- E if ALL THREE names or numbers are DIFFERENT

81.	3457988	3457986	3457986
82.	4695682	4695862	4695682
83.	Stricklund Kanedy	Stricklund Kanedy	Stricklund Kanedy
84.	Joy Harlor Witner	Joy Harloe Witner	Joy Harloe Witner
85.	R. M.O. Uberroth	R. M.O. Uberroth	R. N.O. Uberroth

In questions 86 through 90, find the correct place for the name in the box.

86. Dunlavey, M. Hilary
- A) →
- Dunleavy, Hilary G.
- B) →
- Dunleavy, Hilary K.
- C) →
- Dunleavy, Hilary S.
- D) →
- Dunleavy, Hilery W.
- E) →

87. Yarbrough, Maria
- A) →
- Yabroudy, Margy
- B) →
- Yarboro, Marie
- C) →
- Yarborough, Marina
- D) →
- Yarborough, Mary
- E) →

88. Prouty, Martha
- A) →
- Proutey, Margaret
- B) →
- Proutey, Maude
- C) →
- Prouty, Myra
- D) →
- Prouty, Naomi
- E) →

89. Pawlowicz, Ruth M.
- A) →
- Pawalek, Edward
- B) →
- Pawelek, Flora G.
- C) →
- Pawlowski, Joan M.
- D) →
- Pawtowski, Wanda
- E) →

90. Vanstory, George
- A) →
- Vanover, Eva
- B) →
- VanSwinderen, Floyd
- C) →
- VanSyckle, Harry
- D) →
- Vanture, Laurence
- E) →

GO ON TO THE NEXT COLUMN.

Answers

91. Add: $28 + 35$ — A) 53 B) 62 C) 64 D) 73 E) none of these

92. Subtract: $78 - 69$ — A) 7 B) 8 C) 18 D) 19 E) none of these

93. Multiply: 86×6 — A) 492 B) 506 C) 516 D) 526 E) none of these

94. Divide: $8 \overline{)648}$ — A) 71 B) 76 C) 81 D) 89 E) none of these

95. Add: $97 + 34$ — A) 131 B) 132 C) 140 D) 141 E) none of these

For each question below, find which one of the suggested answers appears in that question.

96. V 5 7 Z N 9 4 T

97. 4 6 P T 2 N K 9

98. 6 4 N 2 P 8 Z K

99. 7 P 5 2 4 N K T

100. K T 8 5 4 N 2 P

Suggested Answers:
- A=2, 5, N, Z
- B=4, 5, N, P
- C=2, 9, P, T
- D=4, 9, T, Z
- E=none of these

GO ON TO THE NEXT PAGE.

In questions 101 through 105, compare the three names or numbers, and mark the answer

A if ALL THREE names or numbers are exactly ALIKE
B if only the FIRST and SECOND names or numbers are exactly ALIKE
C if only the FIRST and THIRD names or numbers are exactly ALIKE
D if only the SECOND and THIRD names or numbers are exactly ALIKE
E if ALL THREE names or numbers are DIFFERENT

101.	1592514	1592574	1592574
102.	2010202	2010202	2010220
103.	6177396	6177936	6177396
104.	Drusilla S. Ridgeley	Drusilla S. Ridgeley	Drusilla S. Ridgeley
105.	Andrei I. Toumantzev	Andrei I. Tourmantzev	Andrei I. Toumantzov

In questions 106 through 110, find the correct place for the name in the box.

106. **Fitzsimmons, Hugh**
- A) →
- Fitts, Harold
- B) →
- Fitzgerald, June
- C) →
- FitzGibbon, Junius
- D) →
- FitzSimons, Martin
- E) →

107. **D'Amato, Vincent**
- A) →
- Daly, Steven
- B) →
- D'Amboise, S. Vincent
- C) →
- Daniel, Vail
- D) →
- DeAlba, Valentina
- E) →

108. **Schaeffer, Roger D.**
- A) →
- Schaffert, Evelyn M.
- B) →
- Schaffner, Margaret M.
- C) →
- Schafhirt, Milton G.
- D) →
- Shafer, Richard E.
- E) →

109. **White-Lewis, Cecil**
- A) →
- Whitelaw, Cordelia
- B) →
- White-Leigh, Nancy
- C) →
- Whitely, Rodney
- D) →
- Whitlock, Warren
- E) →

110. **VanDerHeggen, Don**
- A) →
- VanDemark, Doris
- B) →
- Vandenberg, H. E.
- C) →
- VanDercook, Marie
- D) →
- vanderLinden, Robert
- E) →

GO ON TO THE NEXT COLUMN.

Answers

111. Add: $75 + 49$
A) 124 B) 125 C) 134 D) 225 E) none of these

112. Subtract: $69 - 45$
A) 14 B) 23 C) 24 D) 26 E) none of these

113. Multiply: 36×8
A) 246 B) 262 C) 288 D) 368 E) none of these

114. Divide: $8 \overline{)328}$
A) 31 B) 41 C) 42 D) 48 E) none of these

115. Multiply: 58×9
A) 472 B) 513 C) 521 D) 522 E) none of these

For each question below, find which one of the suggested answers appears in that question.

116. Z 3 N P G 5 4 2

117. 6 N 2 8 G 4 P T

118. 6 N 4 T V G 8 2

119. T 3 P 4 N 8 G 2

120. 6 7 K G N 2 L 5

Suggested Answers
- A=2, 3, G, N
- B=2, 6, N, T
- C=3, 4, G, K
- D=4, 6, K, T
- E=none of these

KEY (CORRECT ANSWERS)

1. B	21. A	41. A	61. C	81. D	101. D
2. E	22. E	42. A	62. B	82. C	102. B
3. D	23. E	43. B	63. E	83. A	103. C
4. A	24. D	44. E	64. E	84. D	104. A
5. E	25. C	45. A	65. C	85. B	105. E
6. E	26. D	46. C	66. A	86. A	106. D
7. A	27. D	47. A	67. D	87. E	107. B
8. D	28. C	48. D	68. C	88. C	108. A
9. B	29. C	49. B	69. D	89. C	109. C
10. E	30. D	50. C	70. E	90. B	110. D
11. D	31. E	51. B	71. A	91. E	111. A
12. B	32. A	52. C	72. C	92. E	112. C
13. B	33. A	53. D	73. B	93. C	113. C
14. B	34. C	54. D	74. C	94. C	114. B
15. B	35. C	55. E	75. A	95. A	115. D
16. A	36. E	56. E	76. D	96. D	116. A
17. D	37. A	57. B	77. D	97. C	117. B
18. E	38. C	58. E	78. A	98. E	118. B
19. B	39. C	59. D	79. E	99. B	119. A
20. A	40. D	60. C	80. C	100. B	120. E

CLERICAL ABILITIES

EXAMINATION SECTION
TEST 1

DIRECTIONS: Each question or incomplete statement is followed by several suggested answers or completions. Select the one that BEST answers the question or completes the statement. *PRINT THE LETTER OF THE CORRECT ANSWER IN THE SPACE AT THE RIGHT.*

Questions 1-4.

DIRECTIONS: Questions 1 through 4 are to be answered on the basis of the information given below.

The most commonly used filing system and the one that is easiest to learn is alphabetical filing. This involves putting records in an A to Z order, according to the letters of the alphabet. The name of a person is filed by using the following order: first, the surname or last name; second, the first name; third, the middle name or middle initial. For example, *Henry C. Young* is filed under *Y* and thereafter under *Young, Henry C.* The name of a company is filed in the same way. For example, *Long Cabinet Co.* is filed under *L,* while *John T. Long Cabinet Co.* is filed under *L* and thereafter under *Long., John T. Cabinet Co.*

1. The one of the following which lists the names of persons in the CORRECT alphabetical order is: 1.____

   A. Mary Carrie, Helen Carrol, James Carson, John Carter
   B. James Carson, Mary Carrie, John Carter, Helen Carrol
   C. Helen Carrol, James Carson, John Carter, Mary Carrie
   D. John Carter, Helen Carrol, Mary Carrie, James Carson

2. The one of the following which lists the names of persons in the CORRECT alphabetical order is: 2.____

   A. Jones, John C.; Jones, John A.; Jones, John P.; Jones, John K.
   B. Jones, John P.; Jones, John K.; Jones, John C.; Jones, John A.
   C. Jones, John A.; Jones, John C.; Jones, John K.; Jones, John P.
   D. Jones, John K.; Jones, John C.; Jones, John A.; Jones, John P.

3. The one of the following which lists the names of the companies in the CORRECT alphabetical order is: 3.____

   A. Blane Co., Blake Co., Block Co., Blear Co.
   B. Blake Co., Blane Co., Blear Co., Block Co.
   C. Block Co., Blear Co., Blane Co., Blake Co.
   D. Blear Co., Blake Co., Blane Co., Block Co.

4. You are to return to the file an index card on *Barry C. Wayne Materials and Supplies Co.* Of the following, the CORRECT alphabetical group that you should return the index card to is 4.____

   A. A to G B. H to M C. N to S D. T to Z

Questions 5-10.

DIRECTIONS: In each of Questions 5 through 10, the names of four people are given. For each question, choose as your answer the one of the four names given which should be filed FIRST according to the usual system of alphabetical filing of names, as described in the following paragraph.

In filing names, you must start with the last name. Names are filed in order of the first letter of the last name, then the second letter, etc. Therefore, BAILY would be filed before BROWN, which would be filed before COLT. A name with fewer letters of the same type comes first; i.e., Smith before Smithe. If the last names are the same, the names are filed alphabetically by the first name. If the first name is an initial, a name with an initial would come before a first name that starts with the same letter as the initial. Therefore, I. BROWN would come before IRA BROWN. Finally, if both last name and first name are the same, the name would be filed alphabetically by the middle name, once again an initial coming before a middle name which starts with the same letter as the initial. If there is no middle name at all, the name would come before those with middle initials or names.

<u>Sample Question:</u> A. Lester Daniels
B. William Dancer
C. Nathan Danzig
D. Dan Lester

The last names beginning with D are filed before the last name beginning with L. Since DANIELS, DANCER, and DANZIG all begin with the same three letters, you must look at the fourth letter of the last name to determine which name should be filed first. C comes before I or Z in the alphabet, so DANCER is filed before DANIELS or DANZIG. Therefore, the answer to the above sample question is B.

5. A. Scott Biala 5.____
B. Mary Byala
C. Martin Baylor
D. Francis Bauer

6. A. Howard J. Black 6.____
B. Howard Black
C. J. Howard Black
D. John H. Black

7. A. Theodora Garth Kingston 7.____
B. Theadore Barth Kingston
C. Thomas Kingston
D. Thomas T. Kingston

8. A. Paulette Mary Huerta 8.____
B. Paul M. Huerta
C. Paulette L. Huerta
D. Peter A. Huerta

9. A. Martha Hunt Morgan 9.____
B. Martin Hunt Morgan
C. Mary H. Morgan
D. Martine H. Morgan

10. A. James T. Meerschaum 10.____
B. James M. Mershum
C. James F. Mearshaum
D. James N. Meshum

Questions 11-14.

DIRECTIONS: Questions 11 through 14 are to be answered SOLELY on the basis of the following information.

You are required to file various documents in file drawers which are labeled according to the following pattern:

DOCUMENTS

MEMOS		LETTERS	
File	Subject	File	Subject
84PM1 - (A-L)		84PC1 - (A-L)	
84PM2 - (M-Z)		84PC2 - (M-Z)	

REPORTS		INQUIRIES	
File	Subject	File	Subject
84PR1 - (A-L)		84PQ1 - (A-L)	
84PR2 - (M-Z)		84PQ2 - (M-Z)	

11. A letter dealing with a burglary should be filed in the drawer labeled 11.____

A. 84PM1 B. 84PC1 C. 84PR1 D. 84PQ2

12. A report on Statistics should be found in the drawer labeled 12.____

A. 84PM1 B. 84PC2 C. 84PR2 D. 84PQ2

13. An inquiry is received about parade permit procedures. It should be filed in the drawer labeled 13.____

A. 84PM2 B. 84PC1 C. 84PR1 D. 84PQ2

14. A police officer has a question about a robbery report you filed. You should pull this file from the drawer labeled 14.____

A. 84PM1 B. 84PM2 C. 84PR1 D. 84PR2

Questions 15-22.

DIRECTIONS: Each of Questions 15 through 22 consists of four or six numbered names. For each question, choose the option (A, B, C, or D) which indicates the order in which the names should be filed in accordance with the following filing instructions:

- File alphabetically according to last name, then first name, then middle initial.
- File according to each successive letter within a name.

- When comparing two names in which, the letters in the longer name are identical to the corresponding letters in the shorter name, the shorter name is filed first.
- When the last names are the same, initials are always filed before names beginning with the same letter.

15. I. Ralph Robinson 15.___
II. Alfred Ross
III. Luis Robles
IV. James Roberts

The CORRECT filing sequence for the above names should be

A. IV, II, I, III
B. I, IV, III, II
C. III, IV, I, II
D. IV, I, III, II

16. I. Irwin Goodwin 16.___
II. Inez Gonzalez
III. Irene Goodman
IV. Ira S. Goodwin
V. Ruth I. Goldstein
VI. M.B. Goodman

The CORRECT filing sequence for the above names should be

A. V, II, I, IV, III, VI
B. V, II, VI, III, IV, I
C. V, II, III, VI, IV, I
D. V, II, III, VI, I, IV

17. I. George Allan 17.___
II. Gregory Allen
III. Gary Allen
IV. George Allen

The CORRECT filing sequence for the above names should be

A. IV, III, I, II
B. I, IV, II, III
C. III, IV, I, II
D. I, III, IV, II

18. I. Simon Kauffman 18.___
II. Leo Kaufman
III. Robert Kaufmann
IV. Paul Kauffmann

The CORRECT filing sequence for the above names should be

A. I, IV, II, III
B. II, IV, III, I
C. III, II, IV, I
D. I, II, III, IV

19. I. Roberta Williams 19.___
II. Robin Wilson
III. Roberta Wilson
IV. Robin Williams

The CORRECT filing sequence for the above names should be

A. III, II, IV, I
B. I, IV, III, II
C. I, II, III, IV
D. III, I, II, IV

20. I. Lawrence Shultz 20.____
II. Albert Schultz
III. Theodore Schwartz
IV. Thomas Schwarz
V. Alvin Schultz
VI. Leonard Shultz

The CORRECT filing sequence for the above names should be

A. II, V, III, IV, I, VI
B. IV, III, V, I, II, VI
C. II, V, I, VI, III, IV
D. I, VI, II, V, III, IV

21. I. McArdle 21.____
II. Mayer
III. Maletz
IV. McNiff
V. Meyer
VI. MacMahon

The CORRECT filing sequence for the above names should be

A. I, IV, VI, III, II, V
B. II, I, IV, VI, III, V
C. VI, III, II, I, IV, V
D. VI, III, II, V, I, IV

22. I. Jack E. Johnson 22.____
II. R.H. Jackson
III. Bertha Jackson
IV. J.T. Johnson
V. Ann Johns
VI. John Jacobs

The CORRECT filing sequence for the above names should be

A. II, III, VI, V, IV, I
B. III, II, VI, V, IV, I
C. VI, II, III, I, V, IV
D. III, II, VI, IV, V, I

Questions 23-30.

DIRECTIONS: The code table below shows 10 letters with matching numbers. For each question, there are three sets of letters. Each set of letters is followed by a set of numbers which may or may not match their correct letter according to the code table. For each question, check all three sets of letters and numbers and mark your answer:

A. if no pairs are correctly matched
B. if only one pair is correctly matched
C. if only two pairs are correctly matched
D. if all three pairs are correctly matched

CODE TABLE

T	M	V	D	S	P	R	G	B	H
1	2	3	4	5	6	7	8	9	0

Sample Question: TMVDSP - 123456
RGBHTM - 789011
DSPRGB - 256789

In the sample question above, the first set of numbers correctly matches its set of letters. But the second and third pairs contain mistakes. In the second pair, M is incorrectly matched with number 1. According to the code table, letter M should be correctly matched with number 2. In the third pair, the letter D is incorrectly matched with number 2. According to the code table, letter D should be correctly matched with number 4. Since only one of the pairs is correctly matched, the answer to this sample question is B.

23. RSBMRM 759262 23.____
GDSRVH 845730
VDBRTM 349713

24. TGVSDR 183247 24.____
SMHRDP 520647
TRMHSR 172057

25. DSPRGM 456782 25.____
MVDBHT 234902
HPMDBT 062491

26. BVPTRD 936184 26.____
GDPHMB 807029
GMRHMV 827032

27. MGVRSH 283750 27.____
TRDMBS 174295
SPRMGV 567283

28. SGBSDM 489542 28.____
MGHPTM 290612
MPBMHT 269301

29. TDPBHM 146902 29.____
VPBMRS 369275
GDMBHM 842902

30. MVPTBV 236194 30.____
PDRTMB 647128
BGTMSM 981232

KEY (CORRECT ANSWERS)

1. A	11. B	21. C
2. C	12. C	22. B
3. B	13. D	23. B
4. D	14. D	24. B
5. D	15. D	25. C
6. B	16. C	26. A
7. B	17. D	27. D
8. B	18. A	28. A
9. A	19. B	29. D
10. C	20. A	30. A

TEST 2

DIRECTIONS: Each question or incomplete statement is followed by several suggested answers or completions. Select the one that BEST answers the question or completes the statement. *PRINT THE LETTER OF THE CORRECT ANSWER IN THE SPACE AT THE RIGHT.*

Questions 1-10.

DIRECTIONS: Questions 1 through 10 each consists of two columns, each containing four lines of names, numbers and/or addresses. For each question, compare the lines in Column I with the lines in Column II to see if they match exactly, and mark your answer A, B, C, or D, according to the following instructions:

A. all four lines match exactly
B. only three lines match exactly
C. only two lines match exactly
D. only one line matches exactly

		COLUMN I	COLUMN II	
1.	I.	Earl Hodgson	Earl Hodgson	1.____
	II.	1409870	1408970	
	III.	Shore Ave.	Schore Ave.	
	IV.	Macon Rd.	Macon Rd.	
2.	I.	9671485	9671485	2.____
	II.	470 Astor Court	470 Astor Court	
	III.	Halprin, Phillip	Halperin, Phillip	
	IV.	Frank D. Poliseo	Frank D. Poliseo	
3.	I.	Tandem Associates	Tandom Associates	3.____
	II.	144-17 Northern Blvd.	144-17 Northern Blvd.	
	III.	Alberta Forchi	Albert Forchi	
	IV.	Kings Park, NY 10751	Kings Point, NY 10751	
4.	I.	Bertha C. McCormack	Bertha C. McCormack	4.____
	II.	Clayton, MO.	Clayton, MO.	
	III.	976-4242	976-4242	
	IV.	New City, NY 10951	New City, NY 10951	
5.	I.	George C. Morill	George C. Morrill	5.____
	II.	Columbia, SC 29201	Columbia, SD 29201	
	III.	Louis Ingham	Louis Ingham	
	IV.	3406 Forest Ave.	3406 Forest Ave.	
6.	I.	506 S. Elliott Pl.	506 S. Elliott Pl.	6.____
	II.	Herbert Hall	Hurbert Hall	
	III.	4712 Rockaway Pkway	4712 Rockaway Pkway	
	IV.	169 E. 7 St.	169 E. 7 St.	

		COLUMN I	COLUMN II	
7.	I.	345 Park Ave.	345 Park Pl.	7.____
	II.	Colman Oven Corp.	Coleman Oven Corp.	
	III.	Robert Conte	Robert Conti	
	IV.	6179846	6179846	
8.	I.	Grigori Schierber	Grigori Schierber	8.____
	II.	Des Moines, Iowa	Des Moines, Iowa	
	III.	Gouverneur Hospital	Gouverneur Hospital	
	IV.	91-35 Cresskill Pl.	91-35 Cresskill Pl.	
9.	I.	Jeffery Janssen	Jeffrey Janssen	9.____
	II.	8041071	8041071	
	III.	40 Rockefeller Plaza	40 Rockafeller Plaza	
	IV.	407 6 St.	406 7 St.	
10.	I.	5971996	5871996	10.____
	II.	3113 Knickerbocker Ave.	3113 Knickerbocker Ave.	
	III.	8434 Boston Post Rd.	8424 Boston Post Rd.	
	IV.	Penn Station	Penn Station	

Questions 11-14.

DIRECTIONS: Questions 11 through 14 are to be answered by looking at the four groups of names and addresses listed below (I, II, III, and IV) and then finding out the number of groups that have their corresponding numbered lines exactly the same.

	GROUP I	GROUP II
Line 1.	Richmond General Hospital	Richman General Hospital
Line 2.	Geriatric Clinic	Geriatric Clinic
Line 3.	3975 Paerdegat St.	3975 Peardegat St.
Line 4	Loudonville, New York 11538	Londonville, New York 11538

	GROUP III	GROUP IV
Line 1.	Richmond General Hospital	Richmend General Hospital
Line 2.	Geriatric Clinic	Geriatric Clinic
Line 3.	3795 Paerdegat St.	3975 Paerdegat St.
Line 4.	Loudonville, New York 11358	Loudonville, New York 11538

11. In how many groups is line one exactly the same? 11.____

    A. Two B. Three C. Four D. None

12. In how many groups is line two exactly the same? 12.____

    A. Two B. Three C. Four D. None

13. In how many groups is line three exactly the same? 13.____

    A. Two B. Three C. Four D. None

14. In how many groups is line four exactly the same? 14.___

A. Two B. Three C. Four D. None

Questions 15-18.

DIRECTIONS: Each of Questions 15 through 18 has two lists of names and addresses. Each list contains three sets of names and addresses. Check each of the three sets in the list on the right to see if they are the same as the corresponding set in the list on the left. Mark your answers:

A. if none of the sets in the right list are the same as those in the left list
B. if only one of the sets in the right list is the same as those in the left list
C. if only two of the sets in the right list are the same as those in the left list
D. if all three sets in the right list are the same as those in the left list

	Left list	Right list	
15.	Mary T. Berlinger 2351 Hampton St. Monsey, N.Y. 20117	Mary T. Berlinger 2351 Hampton St. Monsey, N.Y. 20117	15.___
	Eduardo Benes 473 Kingston Avenue Central Islip, N.Y. 11734	Eduardo Benes 473 Kingston Avenue Central Islip, N.Y. 11734	
	Alan Carrington Fuchs 17 Gnarled Hollow Road Los Angeles, CA 91635	Alan Carrington Fuchs 17 Gnarled Hollow Road Los Angeles, CA 91685	
16.	David John Jacobson 178 35 St. Apt. 4C New York, N.Y. 00927	David John Jacobson 178 53 St. Apt. 4C New York, N.Y. 00927	16.___
	Ann-Marie Calonella 7243 South Ridge Blvd. Bakersfield, CA 96714	Ann-Marie Calonella 7243 South Ridge Blvd. Bakersfield, CA 96714	
	Pauline M. Thompson 872 Linden Ave. Houston, Texas 70321	Pauline M. Thomson 872 Linden Ave. Houston, Texas 70321	
17.	Chester LeRoy Masterton 152 Lacy Rd. Kankakee, Ill. 54532	Chester LeRoy Masterson 152 Lacy Rd. Kankakee, Ill. 54532	17.___
	William Maloney S. LaCrosse Pla. Wausau, Wisconsin 52146	William Maloney S. LaCross Pla. Wausau, Wisconsin 52146	
	Cynthia V. Barnes 16 Pines Rd. Greenpoint, Miss. 20376	Cynthia V. Barnes 16 Pines Rd. Greenpoint, Miss. 20376	

18.	Marcel Jean Frontenac 8 Burton On The Water Calender, Me. 01471	Marcel Jean Frontenac 6 Burton On The Water Calender, Me. 01471	18.____
	J. Scott Marsden 174 S. Tipton St. Cleveland, Ohio	J. Scott Marsden 174 Tipton St. Cleveland, Ohio	
	Lawrence T. Haney 171 McDonough St. Decatur, Ga. 31304	Lawrence T. Haney 171 McDonough St. Decatur, Ga. 31304	

Questions 19-26.

DIRECTIONS: Each of Questions 19 through 26 has two lists of numbers. Each list contains three sets of numbers. Check each of the three sets in the list on the right to see if they are the same as the corresponding set in the list on the left. Mark your answers:

A. if none of the sets in the right list are the same as those in the left list
B. if only one of the sets in the right list is the same as those in the left list
C. if only two of the sets in the right list are the same as those in the left list
D. if all three sets in the right list are the same as those in the left list

19.	7354183476 4474747744 57914302311	7354983476 4474747774 57914302311	19.____
20.	7143592185 8344517699 9178531263	7143892185 8344518699 9178531263	20.____
21.	2572114731 8806835476 8255831246	257214731 8806835476 8255831246	21.____
22.	331476853821 6976658532996 3766042113715	331476858621 6976655832996 3766042113745	22.____
23.	8806663315 74477138449 211756663666	8806663315 74477138449 211756663666	23.____
24.	990006966996 53022219743 4171171117717	99000696996 53022219843 4171171177717	24.____
25.	24400222433004 5300030055000355 20000075532002022	24400222433004 5300030055500355 20000075532002022	25.____

26. 611166640660001116 | 61116664066001116 | 26.____
711130011700110073 | 711130011700110073
26666446664476518 | 26666446664476518

Questions 27-30.

DIRECTIONS: Questions 27 through 30 are to be answered by picking the answer which is in the correct numerical order, from the lowest number to the highest number, in each question.

27. A. 44533, 44518, 44516, 44547 27.____
B. 44516, 44518, 44533, 44547
C. 44547, 44533, 44518, 44516
D. 44518, 44516, 44547, 44533

28. A. 95587, 95593, 95601, 95620 28.____
B. 95601, 95620, 95587, 95593
C. 95593, 95587, 95601, 95620
D. 95620, 95601, 95593, 95587

29. A. 232212, 232208, 232232, 232223 29.____
B. 232208, 232223, 232212, 232232
C. 232208, 232212, 232223, 232232
D. 232223, 232232, 232208, 232212

30. A. 113419, 113521, 113462, 113588 30.____
B. 113588, 113462, 113521, 113419
C. 113521, 113588, 113419, 113462
D. 113419, 113462, 113521, 113588

KEY (CORRECT ANSWERS)

1. C	11. A	21. C
2. B	12. C	22. A
3. D	13. A	23. D
4. A	14. A	24. A
5. C	15. C	25. C
6. B	16. B	26. C
7. D	17. B	27. B
8. A	18. B	28. A
9. D	19. B	29. C
10. C	20. B	30. D

NAME AND NUMBER CHECKING

EXAMINATION SECTION
TEST 1

DIRECTIONS: Questions 1 through 17 consist of sets of names and addresses. In each question, the name and address in Column II should be an exact copy of the name and address in Column I.

If there is:
a mistake only in the name, mark your answer A;
a mistake only in the address, mark your answer B;
a mistake in both name and address, mark your answer C;
NO mistake in either name or address, mark your answer D.

<u>SAMPLE QUESTION</u>

Column I	Column II
Christina Magnusson 288 Greene Street New York, N.Y. 10003	Christina Magnusson 288 Greene Street New York, N.Y. 10013

Since there is a mistake only in the address (the zip code should be 10003 instead of 10013), the answer to the sample question is B.

	<u>COLUMN I</u>	<u>COLUMN II</u>	
1.	Ms. Joan Kelly 313 Franklin Ave. Brooklyn, N.Y. 11202	Ms. Joan Kielly 318 Franklin Ave. Brooklyn, N.Y. 11202	1.____
2.	Mrs. Eileen Engel 47-24 86 Road Queens, N.Y. 11122	Mrs. Ellen Engel 47-24 86 Road Queens, N.Y. 11122	2.____
3.	Marcia Michaels 213 E. 81 St. New York, N.Y. 10012	Marcia Michaels 213 E. 81 St. New York, N.Y. 10012	3.____
4.	Rev. Edward J. Smyth 1401 Brandeis Street San Francisco, Calif. 96201	Rev. Edward J. Smyth 1401 Brandies Street San Francisco, Calif. 962O1	4.____
5.	Alicia Rodriguez 24-68 81 St. Elmhurst, N.Y. 11122	Alicia Rodriguez 2468 81 St. Elmhurst, N.Y. 11122	5.____
6.	Ernest Eisemann 21 Columbia St. New York, N.Y. 10007	Ernest Eisermann 21 Columbia St. New York, N.Y. 10007	6.____

	Column I	COLUMN II	
7.	Mr. & Mrs. George Petersson 87-11 91st Avenue Woodhaven, N.Y. 11421	Mr. & Mrs. George Peterson 87-11 91st Avenue Woodhaven, N.Y. 11421	7.___
8.	Mr. Ivan Klebnikov 1848 Newkirk Avenue Brooklyn, N.Y. 11226	Mr. Ivan Klebikov 1848 Newkirk Avenue Brooklyn, N.Y. 11622	8.___
9.	Samuel Rothfleisch 71 Pine Street New York, N.Y. 10005	Samuel Rothfleisch 71 Pine Street New York, N.Y. 10005	9.___
10.	Mrs. Isabel Tonnessen 198 East 185th Street Bronx, N.Y. 10458	Mrs. Isabel Tonnessen 189 East 185th Street Bronx, N.Y. 10458	10.___
11.	Esteban Perez 173 Eighth Street Staten Island, N.Y. 10306	Estaban Perez 173 Eighth Street Staten Island, N.Y. 10306	11.___
12.	Esta Wong 141 West 68 St. New York, N.Y. 10023	Esta Wang 141 West 68 St. New York, N.Y. 10023	12.___
13.	Dr. Alberto Grosso 3475 12th Avenue Brooklyn, N.Y. 11218	Dr. Alberto Grosso 3475 12th Avenue Brooklyn, N.Y. 11218	13.___
14.	Mrs. Ruth Bortlas 482 Theresa Ct. Far Rockaway, N.Y. 11691	Ms. Ruth Bortlas 482 Theresa Ct. Far Rockaway, N.Y. 11169	14.___
15.	Mr. & Mrs. Howard Fox 2301 Sedgwick Ave. Bronx, N.Y. 10468	Mr. & Mrs. Howard Fox 231 Sedgwick Ave. Bronx, N.Y. 10468	15.___
16.	Miss Marjorie Black 223 East 23 Street New York, N.Y. 10010	Miss Margorie Black 223 East 23 Street New York, N.Y. 10010	16.___
17.	Michelle Herman 806 Valley Rd. Old Tappan, N.J. 07675	Michelle Hermann 806 Valley Dr. Old Tappan, N.J. 07675	17.___

KEY (CORRECT ANSWERS)

1. C
2. A
3. D
4. B
5. B
6. A
7. A
8. C
9. D
10. B
11. A
12. A
13. D
14. C
15. B
16. A
17. C

TEST 2

DIRECTIONS: Questions 1 through 15 are to be answered SOLELY on the instructions given below. *PRINT THE LETTER OF THE CORRECT ANSWER IN THE SPACE AT THE RIGHT.*

INSTRUCTIONS:

In each of the following questions, the 3-line name and address in Column I is the master-list entry, and the 3-line entry in Column 2 is the information to be checked against the master list. If there is one line that does not match, mark your answer A; if there are two lines that do not match, mark your answer B; if all three lines do not match, mark your answer C; if the lines all match exactly, mark your answer D.

SAMPLE QUESTION

Column I	Column II
Mark L. Field	Mark L. Field
11-09 Prince Park Blvd.	11-99 Prince Park Way
Bronx, N.Y. 11402	Bronx, N.Y. 11401

The first lines in each column match exactly. The second lines do not match since 11-09 does not match 11-99; and Blvd. does not match Way. The third lines do not match either since 11402 does not match 11401. Therefore, there are two lines that do not match, and the CORRECT answer is B.

	COLUMN I	COLUMN II	
1.	Jerome A. Jackson 1243 14th Avenue New York, N.Y. 10023	Jerome A. Johnson 1234 14th Avenue New York, N.Y. 10023	1._
2.	Sophie Strachtheim 33-28 Connecticut Ave. Far Rockaway, N.Y. 11697	Sophie Strachtheim 33-28 Connecticut Ave. Far Rockaway, N.Y. 11697	2._
3.	Elisabeth N.T. Gorrell 256 Exchange St. New York, N.Y. 10013	Elizabeth N.T. Gorrell 256 Exchange St. New York, N.Y. 10013	3._
4.	Maria J. Gonzalez 7516 E. Sheepshead Rd. Brooklyn, N.Y. 11240	Maria J. Gonzalez 7516 N. Shepshead Rd. Brooklyn, N.Y. 11240	4._
5.	Leslie B. Brautenweiler 21 57A Seiler Terr. Flushing, N.Y. 11367	Leslie B. Brautenwieler 21-75A Seiler Terr. Flushing, N.J. 11367	5._
6.	Rigoberto J. Peredes 157 Twin Towers, #18F Tottenville, S.I., N.Y.	Rigoberto J. Peredes 157 Twin Towers, #18F Tottenville, S.I., N.Y.	6._

	COLUMN I	COLUMN II	
7.	Pietro F. Albino P.O. Box 7548 Floral Park, N.Y. 11005	Pietro F. Albina P.O. Box 7458 Floral Park, N.Y. 11005	7.____
8.	Joanne Zimmermann Bldg. SW, Room 314 532-4601	Joanne Zimmermann Bldg. SW, Room 314 532-4601	8.____
9.	Carlyle Whetstone Payroll Div.-A, Room 212A 262-5000, ext. 471	Caryle Whetstone Payroll Div.-A, Room 212A 262-5000, ext. 417	9.____
10.	Kenneth Chiang Legal Council, Room 9745 (201) 416-9100, ext. 17	Kenneth Chiang Legal Counsel, Room 9745 (201) 416-9100, ext. 17	10.____
11.	Ethel Koenig Personnel Services Division, Room 433 635-7572	Ethel Hoenig Personal Services Division, Room 433 635-7527	11.____
12.	Joyce Ehrhardt Office of the Administrator, Room W56 387-8706	Joyce Ehrhart Office of the Administrator, Room W56 387-7806	12.____
13.	Ruth Lang EAM Bldg., Room C101 625-2000, ext. 765	Ruth Lang EAM Bldg., Room C110 625-2000, ext. 765	13.____
14.	Anne Marie Ionozzi Investigations, Room 827 576-4000, ext. 832	Anna Marie Ionozzi Investigation, Room 827 566-4000, ext. 832	14.____
15.	Willard Jameson Fm C Bldg., Room 687 454-3010	Willard Jamieson Fm C Bldg., Room 687 454-3010	15.____

KEY (CORRECT ANSWERS)

1. B
2. D
3. A
4. A
5. C
6. D
7. B
8. D
9. B
10. A
11. C
12. B
13. A
14. C
15. A

TEST 3

DIRECTIONS: Questions 1 through 10 are to be answered on the basis of the following instructions. *PRINT THE LETTER OF THE CORRECT ANSWER IN THE SPACE AT THE RIGHT.*

INSTRUCTIONS:

For each such set of names, addresses, and numbers listed in Columns I and II, select your answer from the following options:

A. The names in Columns I and II are different.
B. The addresses in Columns I and II are different.
C. The numbers in Columns I and II are different.
D. The names, addresses, and numbers in Columns I and II are identical.

	COLUMN I	COLUMN II	
1.	Francis Jones 62 Stately Avenue 96-12446	Francis Jones 62 Stately Avenue 96-21446	1.____
2.	Julio Montez 19 Ponderosa Road 56-73161	Julio Montez 19 Ponderosa Road 56-71361	2.____
3.	Mary Mitchell 2314 Melbourne Drive 68-92172	Mary Mitchell 2314 Melbourne Drive 68-92172	3.____
4.	Harry Patterson 25 Dunne Street 14-33430	Harry Patterson 25 Dunne Street 14-34330	4.____
5.	Patrick Murphy 171 West Hosmer Street 93-81214	Patrick Murphy 171 West Hosmer Street 93-18214	5.____
6.	August Schultz 816 St. Clair Avenue 53-40149	August Schultz 816 St. Claire Avenue 53-40149	6.____
7.	George Taft 72 Runnymede Street 47-04033	George Taft 72 Runnymede Street 47-04023	7.____
8.	Angus Henderson 1418 Madison Street 81-76375	Angus Henderson 1418 Madison Street 81-76375	8.____
9.	Carolyn Mazur 12 Riverview Road 38-99615	Carolyn Mazur 12 Rivervane ftoad 38-99615	9.____

	COLUMN I	COLUMN II	
10.	Adele Russell 1725 Lansing Lane 72-91962	Adela Russell 1725 Lansing Lane 72-91962	10.____

KEY (CORRECT ANSWERS)

1.	C	6.	B
2.	C	7.	C
3.	D	8.	D
4.	C	9.	B
5.	C	10.	A

TEST 4

DIRECTIONS: Questions 1 through 20 test how good you are at catching mistakes in typing or printing. In each question, the name and address in Column II should be an exact copy of the name and address in Column I. Mark your answer

A. if there is no mistake in either name or address;
B. if there is a mistake in both name and address;
C. if there is a mistake only in the name;
D. if there is a mistake only in the address.

PRINT THE LETTER OF THE CORRECT ANSWER IN THE SPACE AT THE RIGHT.

	COLUMN I	COLUMN II	
1.	Milos Yanocek 33-60 14 Street Long Island City, N.Y. 11011	Milos Yanocek 33-60 14 Street Long Island City, N.Y. 11001	1.____
2.	Alphonse Sabattelo 24 Minnetta Lane New York, N.Y. 10006	Alphonse Sabbattelo 24 Minetta Lane New York, N.Y. 10006	2.____
3.	Helen Steam 5 Metropolitan Oval Bronx, N.Y. 10462	Helene Stearn 5 Metropolitan Oval Bronx, N.Y. 10462	3.____
4.	Jacob Weisman 231 Francis Lewis Boulevard Forest Hills, N.Y. 11325	Jacob Weisman 231 Francis Lewis Boulevard Forest Hills, N.Y. 11325	4.____
5.	Riccardo Fuente 134 West 83 Street New York, N.Y. 10024	Riccardo Fuentes 134 West 88 Street New York, N.Y. 10024	5.____
6.	Dennis Lauber 52 Avenue D Brooklyn, N.Y. 11216	Dennis Lauder 52 Avenue D Brooklyn, N.Y. 11216	6.____
7.	Paul Cutter 195 Galloway Avenue Staten Island, N.Y. 10356	Paul Cutter 175 Galloway Avenue Staten Island, N.Y. 10365	7.____
8.	Sean Donnelly 45-58 41 Avenue Woodside, N.Y. 11168	Sean Donnelly 45-58 41 Avenue Woodside, N.Y. 11168	8.____
9.	Clyde Willot 1483 Rockaway Avenue Brooklyn, N.Y. 11238	Clyde Willat 1483 Rockway Avenue Brooklyn, N.Y. 11238	9.____

	COLUMN I	COLUMN II	
10.	Michael Stanakis 419 Sheriden Avenue Staten Island, N.Y. 10363	Michael Stanakis 419 Sheraden Avenue Staten Island, N.Y. 10363	10.____
11.	Joseph DiSilva 63-84 Saunders Road Rego Park, N.Y. 11431	Joseph Disilva 64-83 Saunders Road Rego Park, N.Y. 11431	11.____
12.	Linda Polansky 2225 Fenton Avenue Bronx, N.Y. 10464	Linda Polansky 2255 Fenton Avenue Bronx, N.Y. 10464	12.____
13.	Alfred Klein 260 Hillside Terrace Staten Island, N.Y. 15545	Alfred Klein 260 Hillside Terrace Staten Island, N.Y. 15545	13.____
14.	William McDonnell 504 E. 55 Street New York, N.Y. 10103	William McConnell 504 E. 55 Street New York, N.Y. 10108	14.____
15.	Angela Cipolla 41-11 Parson Avenue Flushing, N.Y. 11446	Angela Cipola 41-11 Parsons Avenue Flushing, N.Y. 11446	15.____
16.	Julie Sheridan 1212 Ocean Avenue Brooklyn, N.Y. 11237	Julia Sheridan 1212 Ocean Avenue Brooklyn, N.Y. 11237	16.____
17.	Arturo Rodriguez 2156 Cruger Avenue Bronx, N.Y. 10446	Arturo Rodrigues 2156 Cruger Avenue Bronx, N.Y. 10446	17.____
18.	Helen McCabe 2044 East 19 Street Brooklyn, N.Y. 11204	Helen McCabe 2040 East 19 Street Brooklyn,. N.Y. 11204	18.____
19.	Charles Martin 526 West 160 Street New York, N.Y. 10022	Charles Martin 526 West 160 Street New York, N.Y. 10022	19.____
20.	Morris Rabinowitz 31 Avenue M Brooklyn, N.Y. 11216	Morris Rabinowitz 31 Avenue N Brooklyn, N.Y. 11216	20.____

KEY (CORRECT ANSWERS)

1.	D	11.	B
2.	B	12.	D
3.	C	13.	A
4.	A	14.	B
5.	B	15.	B
6.	C	16.	C
7.	D	17.	C
8.	A	18.	D
9.	B	19.	A
10.	D	20.	D

TEST 5

DIRECTIONS: In copying the addresses below from Column A to the same line in Column B, an Agent-in-Training made some errors. For Questions 1 through 5, if you find that the Agent made an error in

only one line, mark your answer A;
only two lines, mark your answer B;
only three lines, mark your answer C;
all four lines, mark your answer D.

EXAMPLE

Column A	Column B
24 Third Avenue	24 Third Avenue
5 Lincoln Road	5 Lincoln Street
50 Central Park West	6 Central Park West
37-21 Queens Boulevard	21-37 Queens Boulevard

Since errors were made on only three lines, namely the second, third, and fourth, the CORRECT answer is C.

PRINT THE LETTER OF THE CORRECT ANSWER IN THE SPACE AT THE RIGHT.

	Column A	Column B	
1.	57-22 Springfield Boulevard	75-22 Springfield Boulevard	1.___
	94 Gun Hill Road	94 Gun Hill Avenue	
	8 New Dorp Lane	8 New Drop Lane	
	36 Bedford Avenue	36 Bedford Avenue	
2.	538 Castle Hill Avenue	538 Castle Hill Avenue	2.___
	54-15 Beach Channel Drive	54-15 Beach Channel Drive	
	21 Ralph Avenue	21 Ralph Avenue	
	162 Madison Avenue	162 Morrison Avenue	
3.	49 Thomas Street	49 Thomas Street	3.___
	27-21 Northern Blvd.	21-27 Northern Blvd.	
	86 125th Street	86 125th Street	
	872 Atlantic Ave.	872 Baltic Ave.	
4.	261-17 Horace Harding Expwy.	261-17 Horace Harding Pkwy.	4.___
	191 Fordham Road	191 Fordham Road	
	6 Victory Blvd.	6 Victoria Blvd.	
	552 Oceanic Ave.	552 Ocean Ave.	
5.	90-05 38th Avenue	90-05 36th Avenue	5.___
	19 Central Park West	19 Central Park East	
	9281 Avenue X	9281 Avenue X	
	22 West Farms Square	22 West Farms Square	

KEY (CORRECT ANSWERS)

1. C
2. A
3. B
4. C
5. B

TEST 6

Questions 1-10.

DIRECTIONS: For Questions 1 through 10, choose the letter in Column II next to the number which EXACTLY matches the number in Column I. *PRINT THE LETTER OF THE CORRECT ANSWER IN THE SPACE AT THE RIGHT.*

COLUMN I	COLUMN II	
1. 14235	A. 13254 B. 12435 C. 13245 D. 14235	1.____
2. 70698	A. 90768 B. 60978 C. 70698 D. 70968	2.____
3. 11698	A. 11689 B. 11986 C. 11968 D. 11698	3.____
4. 50497	A. 50947 B. 50497 C. 50749 D. 54097	4.____
5. 69635	A. 60653 B. 69630 C. 69365 D. 69635	5.____
6. 1201022011	A. 1201022011 B. 1201020211 C. 1202012011 D. 1021202011	6.____
7. 3893981389	A. 3893891389 B. 3983981389 C. 3983891389 D. 3893981389	7.____
8. 4765476589	A. 4765476598 B. 4765476588 C. 4765476589 D. 4765746589	8.____

COLUMN I	COLUMN II	
9. 8679678938	A. 8679687938	9.____
	B. 8679678938	
	C. 8697678938	
	D. 8678678938	
10. 6834836932	A. 6834386932	10.____
	B. 6834836923	
	C. 6843836932	
	D. 6834836932	

Questions 11-15.

DIRECTIONS: For Questions 11 through 15, determine how many of the symbols in Column Z are exactly the same as the symbol in Column Y.
If none is exactly the same, answer A;
if only one symbol is exactly the same, answer B;
if two symbols are exactly the same, answer C;
if three symbols are exactly the same, answer D.

SYMBOL COLUMN Y	SYMBOL COLUMN Z	
11. A123B1266	A123B1366	11.____
	A123B1266	
	A133B1366	
	A123B1266	
12. CC28D3377	CD22D3377	12.____
	CC38D3377	
	CC28C3377	
	CC28D2277	
13. M21AB201X	M12AB201X	13.____
	M21AB201X	
	M21AB201Y	
	M21BA201X	
14. PA383Y744	AP383Y744	14.____
	PA338Y744	
	PA388Y744	
	PA383Y774	
15. PB2Y8893	PB2Y8893	15.____
	PB2Y8893	
	PB3Y8898	
	PB2Y8893	

KEY (CORRECT ANSWERS)

1. D
2. C
3. D
4. B
5. D
6. A
7. D
8. C
9. B
10. D
11. C
12. A
13. B
14. A
15. D

BASIC FUNDAMENTALS OF FILING SCIENCE

TABLE OF CONTENTS

BASIC FUNDAMENTALS OF FILING SCIENCE

I. COMMENTARY

Filing is the systematic arrangement and storage of papers, cards, forms, catalogues, etc., so that they may be found easily and quickly. The importance of an efficient filing system cannot be emphasized too strongly. The filed materials form records which may be needed quickly to settle questions that may cause embarrassing situations if such evidence is not available. In addition to keeping papers in order so that they are readily available, the filing system must also be designed to keep papers in good condition. A filing system must be planned so that papers may be filed easily, withdrawn easily, and as quickly returned to their proper place. The cost of a filing system is also an important factor.

The need for a filing system arose when the business man began to carry on negotiations on a large scale. He could no longer be intimate with the details of his business. What was needed in the early era was a spindle or pigeon-hole desk. Filing in pigeon-hole desks is now almost completely extinct. It was an unsatisfactory practice since pigeon holes were not labeled, and the desk was an untidy mess.

II. BASIS OF FILING

The science of filing is an exact one and entails a thorough understanding of basic facts, materials, and methods. An overview of this important information now follows.

1. Types of files

(1) SHANNON FILE

This consists of a board, at one end of which are fastened two arches which may be opened laterally.

(2) SPINDLE FILE

This consists of a metal or wood base to which is attached a long, pointed spike. Papers are pushed down on the spike as received. This file is useful for temporary retention of papers.

(3) BOX FILE

This is a heavy cardboard or metal box, opening from the side like a book.

(4) FLAT FILE

This consists of a series of shallow drawers or trays, arranged like drawers in a cabinet.

(5) BELLOWS FILE

This is a heavy cardboard container with alphabetized or compartment sections, the ends of which are closed in such a manner that they resemble an accordion.

(6) VERTICAL FILE

This consists of one or more drawers in which the papers are stood on edge, usually in folders, and are indexed by guides. A series of two or more drawers in one unit is the usual file cabinet.

(7) CLIP FILE

This file has a large clip attached to a board and is very similar to the *SHANNON FILE.*

(8) VISIBLE FILE

Cards are filed flat in an overlapping arrangement which leaves a part of each card visible at all times.

(9) ROTARY FILE

The *ROTARY FILE* has a number of visible card files attached to a post around which they can be revolved. The wheel file has visible cards which rotate around a horizontal axle.

(10) TICKLER FILE

This consists of cards or folders marked with the days of the month, in which materials are filed and turned up on the appropriate day of the month.

2. Aids in filing

(1) GUIDES

Guides are heavy cardboard, pasteboard, or bristol-board sheets the same size as folders. At the top is a tab on which is marked or printed the distinguishing letter, words, or numbers indicating the material filed in a section of the drawer.

(2) SORTING TRAYS

Sorting trays are equipped with alphabetical guides to facilitate the sorting of papers preparatory to placing them in a file.

(3) CODING

Once the classification or indexing caption has been determined, it must be indicated on the letter for filing purposes.

(4) CROSS REFERENCE

Some letters or papers might easily be called for under two or more captions. For this purpose, a cross-reference card or sheet is placed in the folder or in the index.

3. Variations of filing systems

(1) VARIADEX ALPHABETIC INDEX

Provides for more effective expansion of the alphabetic system.

(2) TRIPLE-CHECK NUMERIC FILING

Entails a multiple cross-reference, as the name implies.

(3) VARIADEX FILING

Makes use of color as an aid in filing.

(4) DEWEY DECIMAL SYSTEM

The system is a numeric one used in libraries or for filing library materials in an office. This special type of filing system is used where material is grouped in finely divided categories, such as in libraries. With this method, all material to be filed is divided into ten major groups, from 000 to 900, and then subdivided into tens, units, and decimals.

4. Centralized filing

Centralized filing means keeping the files in one specific or central location. Decentralized filing means putting away papers in files of individual departments. The first step in the organization of a central filing department is to make a careful canvass of all desks in the offices. In this manner we can determine just what material needs to be filed, and what information each desk occupant requires from the central file. Only papers which may be used at some time by persons in the various offices should be placed in the central file. A paper that is to be used at some time by persons in the various offices should be placed in the central file. A paper that is to be used by one department only should never be filed in the central file.

5. Methods of filing

While there are various methods used for filing, actually there are only five basic systems: alphabetical, subject, numerical, geographic, and chronological. All other systems are derived from one of these or from a combination of two or more of them.

Since the purpose of a filing system is to store business records systemically so that any particular record can be found almost instantly when required, filing requires, in addition to the proper kinds of equipment and supplies, an effective method of indexing.

There are five basic systems of filing:

(1) ALPHABETIC FILING

Most filing is alphabetical. Other methods, as described below, require extensive alphabetization.

In alphabetic filing, lettered dividers or guides are arranged in alphabetic sequence. Material to be filed is placed behind the proper guide. All materials under each letter are also arranged alphabetically. Folders are used unless the file is a card index.

(2) SUBJECT FILING

This method is used when a single, complete file on a certain subject is desired. A subject file is often maintained to assemble all correspondence on a certain subject. Such files are valuable in connection with insurance claims, contract negotiations, personnel, and other investigations, special programs, and similar subjects.

(3) GEOGRAPHICAL FILE

Materials are filed according to location: states, cities, counties, or other subdivisions. Statistics and tax information are often filed in this manner.

(4) CHRONOLOGICAL FILE

Records are filed according to date. This method is used especially in "tickler" files that have guides numbered 1 to 31 for each day of the month. Each number indicates the day of the month when the filed item requires attention.

(5) NUMERICAL FILE

This method requires an alphabetic card index giving name and number. The card index is used to locate records numbered consecutively in the files according to date received or sequence in which issued, such as licenses, permits, etc.

6. Indexing

Determining the name or title under which an item is to be filed is known as indexing. For example, how would a letter from Robert E. Smith be filed? The name would be rearranged Smith,Robert E., so that the letter would be filed under the last name.

7. Alphabetizing

The arranging of names for filing is known as alphabetizing. For example, suppose you have four letters indexed under the names Johnson, Becker, Roe, and Stern. How should these letters be arranged in the files so that they may be found easily? You would arrange the four names alphabetically, thus, Becker, Johnson, Roe, and Stern.

III. RULES FOR INDEXING AND ALPHABETIZING

1. The names of persons are to be transposed. Write the surname first, then the given name, and, finally, the middle name or initial. Then arrange the various names according to the alphabetic order of letters throughout the entire name. If there is a title, consider that after the middle name or initial.

NAMES	*INDEXED AS*
Arthur L.Bright	Bright, Arthur L.
Arthur S.Bright	Bright, Arthur S.
P.E. Cole	Cole, P.E.

Dr. John C. Fox	Fox, John C. (Dr.)

2. If a surname includes the same letters of another surname, with one or more additional letters added to the end, the shorter surname is placed first regardless of the given name or the initial of the given name.

NAMES	*INDEXED AS*
Robert E. Brown	Brown, Robert E.
Gerald A. Browne	Browne, Gerald A.
William O. Brownell	Brownell, William O.

3. Firm names are alphabetized under the surnames. Words like the, an, a, of, and for, are not considered.

NAMES	*INDEXED AS*
Bank of America	Bank of America
Bank Discount Dept.	Bank Discount Dept.
The Cranford Press	Cranford Press, The
Nelson Dwyer & Co.	Dwyer, Nelson, & Co.
Sears, Roebuck & Co.	Sears, Roebuck & Co.
Montgomery Ward & Co.	Ward, Montgomery, & Co.

4. The order of filing is determined first of all by the first letter of the names to be filed. If the first letters are the same, the order is determined by the second letters, and so on. In the following pairs of names, the order is determined by the letters underlined:

Austen	Hayes	Hanson	Harvey	Heath	Green	Schwartz
Baker	Heath	Harper	Harwood	Heaton	Greene	Schwarz

5. When surnames are alike, those with initials only precede those with given names, unless the first initial comes alphabetically after the first letter of the name.

Gleason, S.	*but,*	Abbott, Mary
Gleason, S.W.		Abbott, W.B.
Gleason, Sidney		

6. Hyphenated names are treated as if spelled without the hyphen.

Lloyd, Paul N.	Lloyd, Robert
Lloyd-Jones, James	Lloyd-Thomas, A.S.

7. Company names composed of single letters which are not used as abbreviations precede the other names beginning with the same letter.

B & S Garage	E Z Duplicator Co.
B X Cable Co.	Eagle Typewriter Co.
Babbitt, R.N.	Edison Company

8. The ampersand (&)andthe apostrophe (') in firm names are disregarded in alphabetizing.

Nelson & Niller	M & C Amusement Corp.
Nelson, Walter J.	M C Art Assn.
Nelson's Bakery	

9. Names beginning with Mac, Mc, or M' are usually placed in regular order as spelled. Some filing systems file separately names beginning with Mc.

MacDonald, R.J.	Mazza, Anthony
Macdonald, S.B.	McAdam, Wm.
Mace, Wm.	McAndrews, Jerry

10. Names beginning with St. are listed as if the name Saint were spelled in full. Numbered street names and all abbreviated names are treated as if spelled out in full.

Saginaw	Fifth Avenue Hotel	Hart Mfg. Co.
St. Louis	42nd Street Dress Shop	Hart, Martin
St. Peter's Rectory	Hart, Chas.	Hart, Thos.

Sandford	Hart, Charlotte	Hart, Thomas A.
Smith, Wm.	Hart, Jas.	Hart, Thos. R.
Smith, Willis	Hart, Janice	

11. Federal, state, or city departments of government should be placed alphabetically under the governmental branch controlling them.
    - Illinois, State of -- Departments and Commissions
        - Banking Dept.
        - Employment Bureau
    - United States Government Departments
        - Commerce
        - Defense
        - State
        - Treasury
12. Alphabetic order

    Each word in a name is an indexing unit. Arrange the names in alphabetic order by comparing similar units in each name. Consider the second units only when the first units are identical. Consider the third units only when both the first and second units are identical.
13. Single surnames or initials

    A surname, when used alone, precedes the same surname with a first name or initial. A surname with a first initial only precedes a surname with a complete first name. This rule is sometimes stated, "nothing comes before something."
14. Surname prefixes

    A surname prefix is not a separate indexing unit, but it is considered part of the surname. These prefixes include: d', D', Da, de, De, Del, Des, Di, Du, Fitz., La, Le, Mc, Mac, 'c, O', St., Van, Van der, Von, Von der, and others. The prefixes M', Mac, and Mc are indexed and filed exactly as they are spelled.
15. Names of firms

    Names of firms and institutions are indexed and filed exactly as they are written when they do not contain the complete name of an individual.
16. Names of firms containing complete individual names

    When the firm or institution name includes the complete name of an individual, the units are transposed for indexing in the same way as the name of an individual.
17. Article "The"

    When the article <u>the</u> occurs at the beginning of a name, it is placed at the end in parentheses but it is not moved. In both cases, it is not an indexing unit and is disregarded in filing.
18. Hyphenated names

    Hyphenated firm names are considered as separate indexing units. Hyphenated surnames of individuals are considered as one indexing unit; this applies also to hyphenated names of individuals whose complete names are part of a firm name.
19. Abbreviations

    Abbreviations are considered as though the name were written in full; however, single letters other than abbreviations are considered as separate indexing units.
20. Conjunctions, prepositions and firm endings

    Conjunctions and prepositions, such as and, for, in, of, are disregarded in indexing and filing but are not omitted or their order changed when writing names on cards and folders. Firm endings, such as Ltd., Inc., Co., Son, Bros., Mfg., and Corp., are treated as a unit in indexing and filing and are considered as though spelled in full, such as Brothers and Incorporated.

21. One or two words

Names that may be spelled either as one or two words are indexed and filed as one word.

22. Compound geographic names

Compound geographic names are considered as separate indexing and filing units, except when the first part of the name is not an English word, such as the Los in Los Angeles.

23. Titles or degrees of individuals, whether preceding or following the name,are not considered in indexing or filing. They are placed in parentheses after the given name or initial. Terms that designate seniority, such as Jr., Sr., 2d, are also placed in parentheses and are considered for indexing and filing only when the names to be indexed are otherwise identical.

Exception A:

When the name of an individual consists of a title and one name only, such as Queen Elizabeth, it is not transposed and the title is considered for indexing and filing.

Exception B:

When a title or foreign article is the initial word of a firm or association name, it is considered for indexing and filing.

24. Possessives

When a word ends in apostrophe s, the s is not considered in indexing and filing. However, when a word ends in s apostrophe, because the s is part of the original word, it is considered. This rule is sometimes stated, "Consider everything up to the apostrophe. "

25. United States and foreign government names

Names pertaining to the federal government are indexed and filed under United States Government and then subdivided by title of the department, bureau, division, commission, or board. Names pertaining to foreign governments are indexed and filed under names of countries and then subdivided by title of the department, bureau, division, commission, or board. Phrases, such as department of, bureau of, division of, commission of, board of, when used in titles of governmental bodies, are placed in parentheses after the word they modify, but are disregarded in indexing and filing. Such phrases, however, are considered in indexing and filing nongovernmental names.

26. Other political subdivisions

Names pertaining to other political subdivisions, such as states, counties, cities, or towns, are indexed and filed under the name of the political subdivision and then subdivided by the title of the department, bureau, division, commission, or board.

27. Addresses

When the same name appears with different addresses, the names are indexed as usual and arranged alphabetically according to city or town. The State is considered only when there is duplication of both individual or company name and city name. If the same name is located at different addresses within the same city, then the names are arranged alphabetically by streets. If the same name is located at more than one address on the same street, then the names are arranged from the lower to the higher street number.

28. Numbers

Any number in a name is considered as though it were written in words, and it is indexed and filed as one unit.

29. Bank names

Because the names of many banking institutions are alike in several respects, as first National Bank, Second National Bank, etc., banks are indexed and filed first by city location, then by bank name, with the state location written in parentheses and considered only if necessary

30. Married women

The legal name of a married woman is the one used for filing purposes. Legally, a man's surname is the only part of a man's name a woman assumes when she marries. Her legal name, therefore, could be either:

(1) Her own first and middle names together with her husband's surname, or
(2) Her own first name and maiden surname, together with her husband's surname.

Mrs. is placed in parentheses at the end of the name. Her husband's first and middle names are given in parentheses below her legal name.

31. An alphabetically arranged list of names illustrating many difficult points of alphabetizing follows.

COLUMN I

Abbot , W.B.
Abbott, Alice
Allen, Alexander B.
Allen, Alexander B., Inc.
Andersen, Hans
Andersen, Hans E.
Andersen, Hans E., Jr.
Anderson, Andrew Andrews,
George Brown Motor Co., Boston
Brown Motor Co., Chicago
Brown Motor Co., Philadelphia
Brown Motor Co., San Francisco
Dean, Anna
Dean, Anna F.
Dean, Anna Frances
Dean & Co.
Deane-Arnold Apartments
Deane's Pharmacy
Deans, Felix A.
Dean's Studio
Deans, Wm.
Deans & Williams
East Randolph
East St.Louis
Easton, Pa.
Eastport, Me.

COLUMN II

54th St. Tailor Shop
Forstall, W.J.
44th St. Garage
M A Delivery Co.
M & C Amusement Corp.
M C Art Assn.
MacAdam, Wm.
Macaulay, James
MacAulay, Wilson
MacDonald, R.J.
Macdonald, S.B.
Mace, Wm.
Mazza, Anthony
McAdam, Wm.
McAndrews, Jerry
Meade & Clark Co.
Meade, S.T.
Meade, Solomon
Sackett Publishing Co.
Sacks, Robert
St.Andrew Hotel
St.John, Homer W.
Saks, Isaac B.
Stephens, Ira
Stevens, Delevan
Stevens, Delila

IV. OFFICIAL EXAMINATION DIRECTIONS AND RULES

To preclude the possibility of conflicting or varying methods of filing, explicit directions and express rules are given to the candidate before he answers the filing questions on an examination.

The most recent official directions and rules for the filing questions are given immediately hereafter.

OFFICIAL DIRECTIONS

Each of questions ... to ... consists of four(five)names. For each question, select the one of the four(five)names that should be first (second)(third)(last) if the four(five)names were arranged in alphabetical order in accordance with the rules for alphabetical filing given below. Read these rules carefully. Then, for each question, indicate in the correspondingly numbered row on the answer sheet the letter preceding the name that should be first(second)(third)(last) in alphabetical order.

OFFICIAL RULES FOR ALPHABETICAL FILING

Names of Individuals

1. The names of individuals are filed in strict alphabetical order, first according to the last name, then according to first name or initial, and, finally, according to middle name or initial. For example: William Jones precedes George Kirk and Arthur S. Blake precedes Charles M. Blake.
2. When the last names are identical, the one with an initial instead of a first name precedes the one "with a first name beginning with the same initial. For example: J.Green precedes Joseph Green.
3. When identical last names also have identical first names, the one without a middle name or initial precedes the one with a middle name or initial. For example:Robert Jackson precedes both Robert C.Jackson and Robert Chester Jackson.
4. When last names are identical and the first names are also identical, the one with a middle initial precedes the one with a middle name beginning with the same initial. For example: Peter A. Brown precedes Peter Alvin Brown.
5. Prefixes such as De, El, La, and Van are considered parts of the names they precede. For example:Wilfred DeWald precedes Alexander Duval.
6. Last names beginning with "Mac" or "Mc" are filed as spelled.
7. Abbreviated names are treated as if they were spelled out. For example: Jos. is filed as Joseph and Robt. is filed as Robert.
8. Titles and designations such as Dr. ,Mrs., Prof. are disregarded in filing.

Names of Business Organizations

1. The names of business organizations are filed exactly as written, except that an organization bearing the name of an individual is filed alphabetically according to the name of the individual in accordance with the rules for filing names of individuals given above. For example: Thomas Allison Machine Company precedes Northern Baking Company.
2. When numerals occur in a name, they are treated as if they were spelled out. For example: 6 stands for six and 4th stands for fourth.
3. When the following words occur in names, they are disregarded: the, of, and Sample: Choose the name that should be filed *third.*

   (A) Fred Town (2) (C) D. Town (1)
   (B) Jack Towne (3) (D) Jack S.Towne (4)

   The numbers in parentheses indicate the proper alphabetical order in which these names should be filed. Since the name that should be filed third is Jack Towne, the answer is (B).

FILING

EXAMINATION SECTION
TEST 1

DIRECTIONS: Each question from 1 through 10 contains four names. For each question, choose the name that should be *FIRST* if the four names were arranged in alphabetical order in accordance with the Rules for Alphabetical Filing given before. Read these rules carefully. Then, for each question, print in the space at the right the letter before the name that should be *FIRST* in alphabetical order.

SAMPLE QUESTION

A.	Jane Earl	(2)
B.	James A. Earle	(4)
C.	James Earl	(1)
D.	J. Earle	(3)

The numbers in parentheses show the proper alphabetical order in which these names should be filed. Since the name that should be filed *FIRST* is James Earl, the answer to the sample question is C.

1. A. Majorca Leather Goods
   B. Robert Maiorca and Sons
   C. Maintenance Management Corp.
   D. Majestic Carpet Mills

   1.____

2. A. Municipal Telephone Service
   B. Municipal Reference Library
   C. Municipal Credit Union
   D. Municipal Broadcasting System

   2.____

3. A. Robert B. Pierce B. R. Bruce Pierce
   C. Ronald Pierce D. Robert Bruce Pierce

   3.____

4. A. Four Seasons Sports Club
   B. 14 Street Shopping Center
   C. Forty Thieves Restaurant
   D. 42nd St. Theaters

   4.____

5. A. Franco Franceschini B. Amos Franchini
   C. Sandra Franceschia D. Lilie Franchinesca

   5.____

6. A. Chas. A. Levine B. Kurt Levene
   C. Charles Levine D. Kurt E. Levene

   6.____

7. A. Prof. Geo. Kinkaid B. Mr. Alan Kinkaid
   C. Dr. Albert A. Kinkade D. Kincade Liquors Inc.

   7.____

8. A. Department of Public Events 8.____
   B. Office of the Public Administrator
   C. Queensborough Public Library
   D. Department of Public Health

9. A. Martin Luther King, Jr. Towers 9.____
   B. Metro North Plaza
   C. Manhattanville Houses
   D. Marble Hill Houses

10. A. Dr. Arthur Davids 10.____
    B. The David Check Cashing Service
    C. A. C. Davidsen
    D. Milton Davidoff

KEY (CORRECT ANSWERS)

1. C
2. D
3. B
4. D
5. C

6. B
7. D
8. B
9. A
10. B

TEST 2

DIRECTIONS: Each of questions 1 to 10 consists of four names. For each question, select the one of the four names that should be *THIRD* if the four names were arranged in alphabetical order in accordance with the Rules of Alphabetical Filing given before. Read these rules carefully. Then, for each question, print in the space at the right the letter preceding the name that should be *THIRD* in alphabetical order.

SAMPLE QUESTION

A.	Fred Town	(2)
B.	Jack Towne	(3)
C.	D. Town	(1)
D.	Jack S. Towne	(4)

The numbers in parentheses indicate the proper alphabetical order in which these names should be filed. Since the name that should be filed *THIRD* is Jack Towne, the answer is B.

1. A. Herbert Restman B. H. Restman C. Harry Restmore D. H. Restmore 1.____

2. A. Martha Eastwood B. Martha E. Eastwood C. Martha Edna Eastwood D. M. Eastwood 2.____

3. A. Timothy Macalan B. Fred McAlden C. Thomas MacAllister D. Mrs. Frank McAllen 3.____

4. A. Elm Trading Co. 4.____
   B. El Dorado Trucking Corp.
   C. James Eldred Jewelry Store
   D. Eldridge Printing, Inc.

5. A. Edward La Gabriel B. Marie Doris Gabriel C. Marjorie N. Gabriel D. Mrs. Marian Gabriel 5.____

6. A. Peter La Vance B. George Van Meer C. Wallace De Vance D. Leonard Vance 6.____

7. A. Fifth Avenue Book Shop 7.____
   B. Mr. Wm. A. Fifner
   C. 52nd Street Association
   D. Robert B. Fiffner

8. A. Dr. Chas. D. Peterson B. Miss Irene F. Petersen C. Lawrence E. Peterson D. Prof. N. A. Petersen 8.____

9. A. 71st Street Theater B. The Seven Seas Corp. C. 7th Ave. Service Co. D. Walter R. Sevan and Co. 9.____

10. A. Aerol Auto Body, Inc. 10.____
B. AAB Automotive Service Corp.
C. Acer Automotive
D. Alerte Automotive Corp.

KEY (CORRECT ANSWERS)

1. D
2. B
3. B
4. D
5. C
6. D
7. A
8. A
9. C
10. A

TEST 3

DIRECTIONS: Same as for Test 2.

1. A. William Carver B. Howard Cambell C. Arthur Chambers D. Charles Banner 1.____

2. A. Paul Moore B. William Moore C. Paul A. Moore D. William Allen Moore 2.____

3. A. George Peters B. Eric Petersen C. G. Peters D. E. Petersen 3.____

4. A. Edward Hallam B. Jos. Frank Hamilton C. Edward A. Hallam D. Joseph F. Hamilton 4.____

5. A. Theodore Madison B. Timothy McGill C. Thomas MacLane D. Thomas A. Madison 5.____

6. A. William O'Hara B. Arthur Gordon C. James DeGraff D. Anne von Glatin 6.____

7. A. Charles Green B. Chas. T. Greene C. Charles Thomas Greene D. Wm. A. Greene 7.____

8. A. John Foss Insurance Co. B. New World Stove Co. C. 14th Street Dress Shop D. Arthur Stein Paper Co. 8.____

9. A. Gold Trucking Co. B. B. 8th Ave. Garage C. The First National Bank D. The Century Novelty Co. 9.____

10. A. F. L. Doskow B. Natalie S. Doskow C. Samuel B. Doskow D. Arthur G. Doskor 10.____

KEY (CORRECT ANSWERS)

1. A
2. B
3. D
4. D
5. D

6. A
7. C
8. B
9. C
10. B

TEST 4

DIRECTIONS: Each question from 1 through 10 consists of four names. For each question, choose the one of the four names that should be *LAST* if the four names were arranged in alphabetical order in accordance with the Rules for Alphabetical Filing given before. Read these rules carefully. Then, for each question, print in the space at the right the letter before the name that should be *LAST* in alphabetical order.

SAMPLE QUESTION

A.	Jane Earl	(2)
B.	James A. Earle	(4)
C.	James Earl	(1)
D.	J. Earle	(3)

The numbers in parentheses show the proper alphabetical order in which these names should be filed. Since the name that should be filed *LAST* is James A. Earle, the answer to the sample question is B.

1. A. Corral, Dr. Robert B. Carrale, Prof. Robert
   C. Corren, R. D. Corret, Ron 1.____

2. A. Rivera, Ilena B. Riviera, Ilene
   C. Rivere, I. D. Riviera Ice-Cream Co. 2.____

3. A. VonHogel, George B. Volper, Gary
   C. Vonner, G. D. Van Pefel, Gregory 3.____

4. A. David Kallish Stationery Co. 4.____
   B. Emerson Microfilm Company
   C. David Kalder Industrial Engineers Associated
   D. 5th Avenue Office Furniture Co.

5. A. A. Bennet, C. B. Benett, Chuck
   C. Bennet, Chas. D. Bennett, Charles 5.____

6. A. The Board of Higher Education 6.____
   B. National Education Commission
   C. Eakin, Hugh
   D. Nathan, Ellen

7. A. McCloud, I. B. MacGowen, Ian
   C. McGowen, Arthur D. Macale, Sean 7.____

8. A. Devine, Sarah B. Devine, S.
   C. Devine, Sara H. D. Devin, Sarah 8.____

9. A. Milstein, Louis B. Milrad, Abraham P.
   C. Milstein, Herman D. Milstien, Harold G. 9.____

10. A. Herfield, Lester L. B. Herbstman, Nathan
    C. Henricksen, Ole A. D. Herfeld, Burton G. 10.____

KEY (CORRECT ANSWERS)

1. D
2. B
3. C
4. A
5. D
6. B
7. C
8. A
9. D
10. A

TEST 5

DIRECTIONS: Same as for Test 4.

1. A. Francis Lattimore B. H. Latham 1.____
   C. G. Lattimore D. Hugh Latham

2. A. Thomas B. Morgan B. B. Thomas Morgan 2.____
   C. T. Morgan D. Thomas Bertram Morgan

3. A. Lawrence A. Villon B. Chas. Valente 3.____
   C. Charles M. Valent D. Lawrence De Villon

4. A. Alfred Devance B. A. R. D'Amico 4.____
   C. Arnold De Vincent D. A. De Pino

5. A. Dr. Milton A. Bergmann B. Miss Evelyn M. Bergmenn 5.____
   C. Prof. E. N. Bergmenn D. Mrs. L. B. Bergmann

6. A. George MacDougald B. Thomas McHern 6.____
   C. William Macholt D. Frank McHenry

7. A. Third National Bank B. Robt. Tempkin Corp. 7.____
   C. 32nd Street Carpet Co. D. Wm. Templeton, Inc.

8. A. Mary Lobell Art Shop B. John La Marca, Inc 8.____
   C. Lawyers' Guild D. Frank Le Goff Studios

9. A. 9th Avenue Garage B. Jos. Nuren Food Co. 9.____
   C. The New Book Store D. Novelty Card Corp.

10. A. Murphy's Moving & Storage, Inc. 10.____
    B. Mid-Island Van Lines Corporation
    C. Mollone Bros. Moving & Storage, Inc.
    D. McShane Moving & Storage, Inc.

KEY (CORRECT ANSWERS)

1. C
2. D
3. A
4. C
5. B

6. B
7. C
8. A
9. B
10. A

TEST 6

DIRECTIONS: Each question contains four names numbered from 1 through 4 but not necessarily numbered in correct filing order. Answer each question by choosing the letter corresponding to the *CORRECT* filing order of the four names in accordance with the Rules for Alphabetic Filing given before. *PRINT THE LETTER OF THE CORRECT ANSWER IN THE SPACE AT THE RIGHT.*

SAMPLE QUESTION

1. Robert J. Smith   2. R. Jeffrey Smith
3. Dr. A. Smythe   4. Allen R. Smithers

A. 1, 2, 3, 4   B. 3, 1, 2, 4   C. 2, 1, 4, 3   D. 3, 2, 1, 4

Since the correct filing order, in accordance with the above rules, is 2, 1, 4, 3, the correct answer is C.

1. 1. J. Chester VanClief   2. John C. VanClief   1.____
3. J. VanCleve   4. Mary L. Vance

A. 4, 3, 1, 2   B. 4, 3, 2, 1   C. 3, 1, 2, 4   D. 3, 4, 1, 2

2. 1. Community Development Agency   2.____
2. Department of Social Services
3. Board of Estimate
4. Bureau of Gas and Electricity

A. 3, 4, 1, 2   B. 1, 2, 4, 3   C. 2, 1, 3, 4   D. 1, 3, 4, 2

3. 1. Dr. Chas. K. Dahlman   2. F. & A. Delivery Service   3.____
3. Department of Water Supply   4. Demano Men's Custom Tailors

A. 1, 2, 3, 4   B. 1, 4, 2, 3   C. 4, 1, 2, 3   D. 4, 1, 3, 2

4. 1. 48th Street Theater   4.____
2. Fourteenth Street Day Care Center
3. Professor A. Cartwright
4. Albert F. McCarthy

A. 4, 2, 1, 3   B. 4, 3, 1, 2   C. 3, 2, 1, 4   D. 3, 1, 2, 4

5. 1. Frances D'Arcy   2. Mario L. DelAmato   5.____
3. William H. Diamond   4. Robert J. DuBarry

A. 1, 2, 4, 3   B. 2, 1, 3, 4   C. 1, 2, 3, 4   D. 2, 1, 3, 4

6. 1. Evelyn H. D'Amelio   2. Jane R. Bailey   6.____
3. Robert Bailey   4. Frank Baily

A. 1, 2, 3, 4   B. 1, 3, 2, 4   C. 2, 3, 4, 1   D. 3, 2, 4, 1

7. 1. Department of Markets   7.____
2. Bureau of Handicapped Children
3. Housing Authority Administration Building
4. Board of Pharmacy

A. 2,1,3,4 B. 1,2,4,3 C. 1,2,3,4 D. 3,2,1,4

8. 1. William A. Shea Stadium 8.____
2. Rapid Speed Taxi Co.
3. Harry Stampler's Rotisserie
4. Wilhelm Albert Shea

A. 2, 3, 4, 1 B. 4, 1, 3, 2 C. 2, 4, 1, 3 D. 3, 4, 1, 2

9. 1. Robert S. Aaron, M. D. 2. Mrs. Norma S. Aaron 9.____
3. Irving I. Aronson 4. Darius P. Aanonsen

A. 1, 2, 3, 4 B. 2, 4, 1, 3 C. 4, 2, 3, 1 D. 4, 2, 1, 3

10. 1. The Gamut 2. Gilliar Drug Co., Inc. 10.____
3. Georgette Cosmetology 4. Great Nock Pharmacy

A. 1, 3, 2, 4 B. 3, 1, 4, 2 C. 1, 2, 3, 4 D. 1, 3, 4, 2

KEY (CORRECT ANSWERS)

1. A
2. D
3. B
4. D
5. C

6. D
7. D
8. C
9. D
10. A

TEST 7

DIRECTIONS: Each question consists of four names grouped vertically under four different filing arrangements lettered A, B, C, and D. In each question only one of the four arrangements lists the names in the correct filing order according to the Rules for Alphabetical Filing given before. Read these rules carefully. Then, for each question, select the correct filing arrangement, lettered A, B, C, or D and print in the space at the right the letter of that correct filing arrangement.

SAMPLE QUESTION

Arrangement A	*Arrangement B*	*Arrangement C*	*Arrangement D*
Arnold Robinson	Arthur Roberts	Arnold Robinson	Arthur Roberts
Arthur Roberts	J. B. Robin	Arthur Roberts	James Robin
J. B. Robin	James Robin	James Robin	J. B. Robin
James Robin	Arnold Robinson	J. B. Robin	Arnold Robinson

Since, in this sample, *ARRANGEMENT B* is the only one in which the four names are correctly arranged alphabetically, the answer is B.

1. *Arrangement A*
Alice Thompson
Arnold G. Thomas
B. Thomas
Eugene Thompkins
Arrangement B
Eugene Thompkins
Alice Thompson
Arnold G. Thomas
B. Thomas
Arrangement C
B. Thomas Arnold
G. Thomas
Eugene Thompkins
Alice Thompson
Arrangement D
Arnold G. Thomas
B. Thomas
Eugene Thompkins
Alice Thompson
1.____

2. *Arrangement A*
Albert Green
A. B. Green
Frank E. Green
Wm. Greenfield
Arrangement B
A. B. Green
Albert Green
Frank E. Green
Wm. Greenfield
Arrangement C
Albert Green
Wm. Greenfield
A. B. Green
Frank E. Green
Arrangement D
A. B. Green
Frank E. Green
Albert Green
Wm. Greenfield
2.____

3. *Arrangement A*
Steven M. Comte
Robt. Count
Robert B. Count
Steven Le Comte
Arrangement B
Steven Le Comte
Steven M. Comte
Robert B. Count
Robt. Count
Arrangement C
Steven M. Comte
Steven Le Comte
Robt. Count
Robert B. Count
Arrangement D
Robt. Count
Robert B. Count
Steven Le Comte
Steven M. Comte
3.____

4. *Arrangement A*
Prof. David Towner
Miss Edna Tower
Dr. Frank I. Tower
Mrs. K. C. Towner

Arrangement B
Dr. Frank I. Tower
Miss Edna Tower
Mrs. K. C. Towner
Prof. David Towner

Arrangement C
Miss Edna Tower
Dr. Frank I. Tower
Prof. David Towner
Mrs. K. C. Towner

Arrangement D
Prof. David Towner
Mrs. K. C. Towner
Miss Edna Tower
Dr. Frank I. Tower

4.____

5. *Arrangement A*
The Jane Miller Shop
Joseph Millard Corp.
John Muller & Co.
Jean Mullins, Inc.

Arrangement B
Joseph Millard Corp.
The Jane Miller Shop
John Muller & Co.
Jean Mullins, Inc.

Arrangement C
The Jane Miller Shop
Jean Mullins, Inc.
John Muller & Co.
Joseph Millard Corp.

Arrangement D
Joseph Millard Corp.
John Muller & Co.
Jean Mullins, Inc.
The Jane Miller Shop

5.____

6. *Arrangement A*
Anthony Delaney
A. M. D'Elia
A. De Landri
Alfred De Monte

Arrangement B
Anthony Delaney
A. De Landri
A. M. D'Elia
Alfred De Monte

Arrangement C
A. De Landri
A. M. D'Elia
Alfred De Monte
Anthony Delaney

Arrangement D
A. De Landri
Anthony Delaney
A. M. D'Elia
Alfred De Monte

6.____

7. *Arrangement A*
D. McAllen
Lewis McBride
Doris MacAllister
Lewis T. Mac Bride

Arrangement B
D. McAllen
Doris MacAllister
Lewis McBride
Lewis T. MacBride

Arrangement C
Doris MacAllister
Lewis T. MacBride
D. McAllen
Lewis McBride

Arrangement D
Doris MacAllister
D. McAllen
Lewis T. MacBride
Lewis McBride

7.____

8. *Arrangement A*
6th Ave. Swim Shop
The Sky Ski School
Sport Shoe Store
23rd Street Salon
Arrangement B
23rd Street Salon
The Sky Ski School
6th Ave. Swim Shop
Sport Shoe Store
Arrangement C
6th Ave. Swim Shop
Sport Shoe Store
The Sky Ski School
23rd Street Salon
Arrangement D
The Sky Ski School
6th Ave. Swim Shop
Sport Shoe Store
23rd Street Salon

8._____

9. *Arrangement A*
Charlotte Stair
C. B. Stare
Charles B. Stare
Elaine La Stella
Arrangement B
C. B. Stare
Charles B. Stare
Charlotte Stair
Elaine La Stella
Arrangement C
Elaine La Stella
Charlotte Stair
C. B. Stare
Charles B. Stare
Arrangement D
Charles B. Stare
C. B. Stare
Charlotte Stair
Elaine La Stella

9._____

10. *Arrangement A*
John O'Farrell Corp.
Finest Glass Co.
George Fraser Co.
4th Guarantee Bank
Arrangement B
Finest Glass Co.
4th Guarantee Bank
George Fraser Co.
John O'Farrell Corp.
Arrangement C
John O'Farrell Corp.
Finest Glass Co.
4th Guarantee Bank
George Fraser Co.
Arrangement D
Finest Glass Co.
George Fraser Co.
John O'Farrell Corp.
4th Guarantee Bank

10._____

KEY (CORRECT ANSWERS)

1. D
2. B
3. A
4. C
5. B

6. D
7. C
8. A
9. C
10. B

TEST 8

DIRECTIONS: Same as for Test 7.

	Arrangement A	*Arrangement B*	*Arrangement C*	
1.	R. B. Stevens Chas. Stevenson Robert Stevens,Sr. Alfred T. Stevens	Alfred T. Stevens R. B. Stevens Robert Stevens,Sr. Chas. Stevenson	R. B. Stevens Robert Stevens,Sr. Alfred T. Stevens Chas. Stevenson	1.____
2.	Mr. A. T. Breen Dr. Otis C. Breen Amelia K.Brewington John Brewington	John Brewington Amelia K.Brewington Dr. Otis C. Breen Mr. A. T. Breen	Dr. Otis C. Breen Mr. A. T. Breen John Brewington Amelia K.Brewington	2.____
3.	J. Murphy J. J. Murphy John Murphy John J. Murphy	John Murphy John J. Murphy J. Murphy J. J. Murphy	J. Murphy John Murphy J. J. Murphy John J. Murphy	3.____
4.	Anthony DiBuono George Burns,Sr. Geo. T. Burns,Jr. Alan J. Byrnes	Geo. T. Burns,Jr. George Burns,Sr. Anthony DiBuono Alan J. Byrnes	George Burns,Sr. Geo. T. Burns, Jr. Alan J. Byrnes Anthony DiBuono	4.____
5.	James Macauley Frank A. McLowery Francis MacLaughry Bernard J. MacMahon	James Macauley Francis MacLoughry Bernard J. MacMahon Frank A. McLowery	Bernard J. MacMahon Francis MacLaughry Frank A. McLowery James Macauley	5.____
6.	A.J. DiBartolo,Sr. A. P. DiBartolo J. A. Bartolo Anthony J. Bartolo	J. A. Bartolo Anthony J. Bartolo A. P. DiBartolo A. J. DiBartolo,Sr.	Anthony J. Bartolo J. A. Bartolo A. J. DiBartolo, Sr. A. P. DiBartolo	6.____
7.	Edward Holmes Corp. Hillside Trust Corp Standard Insurance Co. The Industrial Surety Co.	Edward Holmes Corp. Hillside Trust Corp. The Industrial Surety Co. Standard Insurance Co.	Hillside TrustCorp. Edward Holmes Corp. The Industrial Surety Co. Standard InsuranceCo.	7.____
8.	Cooperative Credit Co. Chas. Cooke Chemical Corp. John Fuller Baking Co. 4th Avenue Express Co.	Chas. Cooke Chemical Corp. Cooperative Credit Co. 4th Avenue Express Co. John Fuller Baking Co.	4th Avenue Express Co. John Fuller Baking Co. Chas. Cooke Chemical Corp. Cooperative CreditCo.	8.____

9.	Mr. R. McDaniels Robert Darling, Jr. F. L. Ramsey Charles DeRhone	F. L. Ramsey Mr. R. McDaniels Charles DeRhone Robert Darling, Jr.	Robert Darling, Jr. Charles DeRhone Mr. R. McDaniels F. L. Ramsey	9._____
10.	New York Omnibus Corp. New York Shipping Co. Nova Scotia Canning Co. John J. O'Brien Co.	John J. O'Brien Co. New York Omnibus Corp. New York Shipping Co. Nova Scotia Caning Co.	Nova Scotia Canning Co. John J. O'Brien Co. New York Omnibus Corp. New York Shipping Co.	10._____

KEY (CORRECT ANSWERS)

1. B
2. A
3. A
4. C
5. B

6. C
7. C
8. B
9. C
10. A

TEST 9

DIRECTIONS: Each question consists of a group of names. Consider each group of names as a unit. Determine in what position the name printed in *ITALICS* would be if the names in the group were *CORRECTLY* arranged in alphabetical order. If the name in *ITALICS* should be first, print the letter A; if second, print the letter B; if third, print the letter C; if fourth, print the letter D; and if fifth, print the letter E. *PRINT THE LETTER OF THE CORRECT ANSWER IN THE SPACE AT THE RIGHT.*

SAMPLE QUESTION

J. W. Martin	2
James E. Martin	4
J. Martin	1
George Martins	5
James Martin	3

1. Albert Brown
James Borenstein
Frieda Albrecht
Samuel Brown
George Appelman
1.____

2. James Ryan
Francis Ryan
Wm. Roanan
Frances S. Ryan
Francis P. Ryan
2.____

3. Norman Fitzgibbons
Charles F. Franklin
Jas. Fitzgerald
Andrew Fitzsimmons
James P. Fitzgerald
3.____

4. Hugh F. Martenson
A. S. Martinson
Albert Martinsen
Albert S. Martinson
M. Martanson
4.____

5. Aaron M. Michelson
Samuel Michels
Arthur L. Michaelson, Sr.
John Michell
Daniel Michelsohn
5.____

6. *Chas. R. Connolly* 6.____
   Frank Conlon
   Charles S. Connolly
   Abraham Cohen
   Chas. Conolly

7. James McCormack 7.____
   Ruth MacNamara
   Kathryn McGillicuddy
   Frances Mason
   Arthur MacAdams

8. Dr. Francis Karell 8.____
   John Joseph Karelsen,
   Jr. John J.Karelsen,Sr.
   Mrs. Jeanette Kelly
   Estelle Karel

9. *The 5th Ave. Bus Co.* 9.____
   The Baltimore and Ohio Railroad
   3rd Ave. Elevated Co.
   Pennsylvania Railroad
   The 4th Ave. Trolley Line

10. Murray B. Cunitz 10.____
    Cunningham Duct Cleaning Corp.
    James A. Cunninghame
    Jason M. Cuomor
    Talmadge L. Cummings

KEY (CORRECT ANSWERS)

1. E
2. D
3. A
4. E
5. D

6. C
7. C
8. D
9. B
10. C

TEST 10

DIRECTIONS: A supervisor who is responsible for the proper maintenance and operation of the filing system in an office of a depart-ment should be able to instruct and guide his subordinates in the correct filing of office records. The following ques-tions,1 through 10, are designed to determine whether you can interpret and follow a prescribed filing procedure. These questions should be answered SOLELY on the basis of the fil-ing instructions which follow.

FILING INSTRUCTIONS FOR PERSONNEL DIVISION DEPARTMENT X

The filing system of this division consists of three separate files, namely: (1) Employee File, (2) Subject File, (3) Correspondence File.

Employee File

This file contains a folder for each person currently employed in the department. Each report, memorandum, and letter which has been received from an official or employee of the department and which pertions to one employee only should be placed in the Employee File folder of the employee with whom the communication is concerned. (Note: This filing procedure also applies to a communication from a staff member who writes on a matter which concerns himself only.)

Subject File

Reports and memoranda originating in the department and dealing with personnel matters affecting the entire staff or certain categories or groups of employees should be placed in the Subject File under the appropriate subject headings. The materials in this file are subdivided under the following five subject headings:

(1) Classification -- includes material on job analysis, change of title, reclassification of positions, etc.

(2) Employment -- includes material on appointment, promotion, re-instatement, and transfer.

(3) Health and Safety -- includes material dealing chiefly with the health and safety of employees.

(4) Staff Regulations -- includes material pertaining to rules and regulations governing such working conditions as hours of work, lateness, vacation, leave of absence, etc.

(5) Training -- includes all material relating to employee training.

Correspondence File

All correspondence received from outside agencies, both public and private, and from persons outside the department, should be placed in the Correspondence File and cross referenced as follows:

(1) When letters from outside agencies or persons relate to one or more employees currently employed in the department, a cross reference sheet should be placed in the Employee File folder of each employee mentioned.

(2) When letters from outside agencies or persons do not mention a specific employee or specific employees of the department, a cross reference sheet should be placed in the Subject File under the appropriate subject heading.

Questions 1-10 describe communications which have been received and acted upon by the Personnel Division of Department X, and which must be filed in accordance with the Filing Instructions for the Personnel Division.

The following filing operations may be performed in accordance with the above filing instructions:

(A) Place in Employee File
(B) Place in Subject File under Classification
(C) Place in Subject File tinder Employment
(D) Place in Subject File under Health and Safety
(E) Place in Subject File under Staff Regulations
(F) Place in Subject File under Training
(G) Place in Correspondence File and cross reference in Employee File
(H) Place in Correspondence File and cross reference in Subject File under Classification
(I) Place in Correspondence File and cross reference in Subject File under Employment
(J) Place in Correspondence File and cross reference in Subject File under Health and Safety
(K) Place in Correspondence File and cross reference in Subject File under Staff Regulations
(L) Place in Correspondence File and cross reference in Subject File under Training

DIRECTIONS: Examine each of questions 1 through 10 carefully. Then, in the space at the right, *print* the capital letter preceding the one of the filing operations listed above which MOST accurately carries out the Filing Instructions for the Personnel Division.

SAMPLE: A Clerk, Grade 2, in the department has sent in a memorandum requesting information regarding the amount of vacation due him.
The CORRECT answer is A.

1. Mr. Clark, a Clerk, Grade 5, has submitted an intradepartmental memorandum that the titles of all Clerks, Grade 5, in the department be changed to Administrative Assistant. 1.____

2. The secretary to the department has issued a staff order revising the schedule of Saturday work from a one-in-two to a one-in-four schedule. 2.____

3. The personnel officer of another agency has requested the printed transcripts of an in-service course recently conducted by the department. 3.____

4. Mary Smith, a secretary to one of the division chiefs, has sent in a request for a maternity leave of absence to begin on April 1 of this year and to terminate on March 31 of next year. 4.____

5. A letter has been received from a civic organization stating that they would like to know how many employees were promoted in the department during the last fiscal year. 5.____

6. The attorney for a municipal employees' organization has requested permission to represent Mr.James Roe, a departmental employee who is being brought up on charges of violating departmental regulations. 6.____

7. A letter has been received from Mr. Wright, a salesman for a paper company, who complains that Miss Jones, an information clerk in the department, has been rude and impertinent and has refused to give him information which should be available to the public. 7.____

8. Helen Brown, a graduate of Commercial High School, has sent a letter inquiring about an appointment as a provisional typist. 8.____

9. The National Office Managers' Society has sent a request to the department for information on its policies on tardiness and absenteeism. 9.____

10. A memorandum has been received from a division chief who states that employees in his unit have complained that their rest room is in a very unsanitary condition. 10.____

KEY (CORRECT ANSWERS)

1. B
2. E
3. L
4. A
5. I

6. G
7. G
8. I
9. K
10. D

FILING

EXAMINATION SECTION
TEST 1

DIRECTIONS: For each of the following, you are given a name above and three other names in alphabetical order below. The letters A, B, C, and D stand for spaces where you could file the name. Find the CORRECT space for the name given above so that it will be in alphabetical order with the names below it. The letter that stands for that space is the answer to the question.

1. CURRAN, THOMAS 1.____
A CURLEY, MARY B CURR, SAMUEL C CURREN, KATIE D

2. KAPLIN, EDWIN 2.____
A KAPLEN, MICHAEL B KAPLIN, JULIA C KAPLON, DAVID D

3. PENSKY, LEONA 3.____
A PENSLER, SANDY B PENSLEY, JOEL C PENSLEY, JOSEPH D

4. ROWEN, MARCIA 4.____
A ROWEN, CHRISTOPHER B ROWEN, LOUIS C ROWEN, MARTIN D

5. FOSTER, GRACE 5.____
A FOSS, EARL B FOSSE, NICHOLE C FOSTER, KEITH D

6. KO, FAI 6.____
A KO, HOK B KO, HUNG-FAI C KO, HYUN JUNG D

7. MICHALIK, ANTHONY 7.____
A MICHALIC, GARY B MICHALIS, HELEN C MICHALK, KLAUS D

8. MINTZ, JUDITH 8.____
A MINTZ, JAKE B MINTZ, JAMES C MINTZ, JULIUS D

9. POWERS, ANN 9.____
A POUST, THERESE B POWELL, LUTHER C POWER, RACHEL D

10. PRACTICAL STUDIO, INC. 10.____
A PRACTICAL PUBLISHING B PRACTICE DEVELOPMENT C PRACTICE SERVICE CORP. D

11. SHERWIN, ROBERTA 11.____
A SHERWIN, RAUL B SHERWIN, RICHARD C SHERWIN, ROBERT D

12. JACOBSEN, JENNIFER 12.____
A JACOBSON, PETER B JACOBY, JACK C JACOVITZ, GAIL D

13. BLEINHEIM, GLORIA 13.____
A BLELOCK, JULIA B BLENCOWE, FRED C BLENMAN, ANTHONY D

14. FIRST STERLING CORP. 14.____
A FIRST STATE PRODUCTS B FIRST STEP INC. C FIRST STOP CORP. D

15. VICKERS, GEORGE 15.____
A VICHEY, LOUIS B VICHI, MARIO C VICKI, SUSAN D

16. STEIN, DAVID 16.____
A STEIN, CRAIG B STEIN, DANIEL C STEIN, DEBORAH D

17. IGLESIAS, BERNADETTE 17.____
A IGER, MARTIN B IGLEHEART, PHYLICIA C IGLEWSKI, RICHARD D

18. IDEAL ROOFING CORP. 18.____
A IDEAL REPRODUCTION B IDEAL RESTAURANT C IDEAL RUBBER PRODUCTS D

19. TODARO, JOSEPH 19.____
A TODD, ANNE B TODE, WALLY C TODMAN, JUDITH D

20. WILKERSON, RUTH 20.____
A WILKENS, FRANK B WILKES, BARRY C WILKIE, JANE D

21. HUGHES, MARY 21.____
A HUGHES, MANUEL B HUGHES, MARGARET C HUGHES, MARTHA D

22. GODWIN, JAMES 22.____
A GODFREY, SONDRA B GODMAN, GABRIEL C GODREAU, ROBERT D

23. NACHMAN, DAVID 23.____
A NACHT, JAMES B NACK, SAUL C NACKENSON, LORI D

24. CASPER, LAURENCE 24.____
A CASPER, LEONARD B CASPER, LESTER C CASPER, LINDA D

25. CULEN, ELLEN 25.____
A CULHANE, JOHN B CULICHI, RADU C CULIN, TERRY D

KEY (CORRECT ANSWERS)

1. C
2. B
3. A
4. C
5. C
6. A
7. B
8. C
9. D
10. B
11. D
12. A
13. A
14. C
15. C
16. C
17. C
18. C
19. A
20. B
21. D
22. D
23. A
24. A
25. A

TEST 2

DIRECTIONS: For each of the following, you are given a name above and three other names in alphabetical order below. The letters A, B, C, and D stand for spaces where you could file the name. Find the CORRECT space for the name given above so that it will be in alphabetical order with the names below it. The letter that stands for that space is the answer to the question.

1. HARMAN, HENRY 1.____
A HARLEY, LILLIAN B HARMER, RALPH C HARMON, CECIL D

2. MANNING, JOHNSON 2.____
A MANNING, JAMES B MANNING, JEROME C MANNING, JOHN D

3. NOGUCHI, JANICE 3.____
A NOEL, WALTER B NOGUET, DANIELLE C NOH, DAVID D

4. PARRON, ALFONSE 4.____
A PARRIS, LEON B PARRISH, LINDA C PARROTT, BETTY D

5. GROSS, ELANA 5.____
A GROSS, ELAINE B GROSS, ELIZABETH C GROSS, ELLIOT D

6. HORSTMANN, ANNA 6.____
A HORSMAN, ALLAN B HORST, VALERIE C HORSTMAN, JAMES D

7. JONES, EMILY 7.____
A JONES, ELMA B JONES, ELOISE C JONES, EMMA D

8. LESSING, FRED 8.____
A LESSER, MARTHA B LESSIN, ELLIE C LESSNER, ERWIN D

9. ROSENBLUM, JULIUS 9.____
A ROSENBLUTH, SYLVIA B ROSENBORG, ERIC C ROSENBURG, JANE D

10. YOUNG, THEODORE 10.____
A YOUNG, TERRY B YOUNG, THELMA C YOUNG, THOMAS D

11. RENICK, KAREN 11.____
A RENIE, JOSEPH B RENITA, JOSE C RENKO, DORIS D

12. ADLER, HELEN 12.____
A ADLER, HAROLD B ADLER, HARRY C ADLER, HENRY D

13. BURKHARDT, ANN 13.____
A BURKET, HARRIET B BURKHOLDER, CARL C BURKHOLZ, SCOTT D

14. DE LUCA, PAUL 14.____
A DE LUCA, JOHN B DE LUCIA, AUDREY C DE LUCIA, ROBERT D

15. DEMBSKI, STEPHEN 15.____
A DEMBLING, JOAN B DEMBNER, PETER C DEMBROW, HELEN D

16. FLYNN, ARCHIE 16.____
A FLYNN, AGNES B FLYNN, ANDREW C FLYNN, ANNMARIE D

17. GRAFFY, PAUL 17.____
A GRAFMAN, ANDREW B GRAFSTEIN, BETTY C GRAFTON, MELVIN D

18. KERMIT, FRANK 18.____
A KERMAN, LINDA B KERMISH, RHODA C KERMOYAN, MICKI D

19. METZLER, MAURICE 19.____
A METZGER, ALFRED B METZIER, SONIA C METZINGER, PAUL D

20. PADDINGTON, TIMOTHY 20.____
A PADDEN, MICHAEL B PADDISON, BRUCE C PADELL, EUNICE D

21. RICHARDSON, BLANCHE 21.____
A RICHARDSON, BETTY B RICHARDSON, BEVERLY C RICHARDSON, BRENDA D

22. ISEKI, EMILE 22.____
A ISELIN, CAROL B ISEN, RICHARD C ISENEE, CYNTHIA D

23. CONNELL, EUGENE 23.____
A CONNELL, EDWARD B CONNELL, HELEN C CONNELL, HUGH D

24. MAC LEOD, LAURIE 24.____
A MAC LEOD, LORNA B MC LANE, PAUL C MC LAREN, DUNCAN D

25. BOLE, KENNETH 25.____
A BOLDEN, ROSIE B BOLDT, LINDA C BOLELLA, DENNIS D

KEY (CORRECT ANSWERS)

1. B
2. D
3. B
4. C
5. B

6. D
7. C
8. C
9. A
10. C

11. A
12. C
13. B
14. B
15. D

16. D
17. A
18. C
19. D
20. B

21. C
22. A
23. B
24. A
25. C

TEST 3

DIRECTIONS: For each of the following, you are given a name above and three other names in alphabetical order below. The letters A, B, C, and D stand for spaces where you could file the name. Find the CORRECT space for the name given above so that it will be in alphabetical order with the names below it. The letter that stands for that space is the answer to the question.

1. CARLISLE, ALAN 1.____
A CARLINSKY, LEONA B CARLITOS, JUAN C CARLL, CHARLES D

2. COLLINS, KAREN 2.____
A COLLINS, KATHLEEN B COLLINS, KATHRYN C COLLINS, KAY D

3. GALLOTTI, OSCAR 3.____
A GALLONTY, FRANCIS B GALLOP, LILLIAN C GALLOU, ALEXIS D

4. MAHADY, JOHN 4.____
A MAHADEO, PRATAB B MAHAJAN, ASHA C MAHARAJAH, MIARIAM D

5. WINGATE, REBECCA 5.____
A WINGARD, LUCILLE B WINGAT, ROBERT C WINGER, HOLLY D

6. ZWEIGHAFT, FREDA 6.____
A ZWEIG, BERTRAM B ZWEIGBAUM, BENJAMIN C ZWEIGENTHAL, DOROTHY D

7. MAXWELL, GEORGE 7.____
A MAXWELL, EDWARD B MAXWELL, FRANK C MAXWELL, HARRIS D

8. O 'DOHERTY, SALLY 8.____
A ODETTE, CHARLES B ODIOTTI, MASSIE C ODNORALOV, MIKHAEL D

9. JAMES, ROGER 9.____
A JAMIESON, KELLY B JAMNER, ELIZABETH C JAMPOLSKY, MILTON D

10. PADIN, FRANCIS 10.____
A PADILLA, ANGELA B PADINGER, JENNY C PADLEY, RAYMOND D

11. AAARMAN, ALEC 11.____
A AABY, JANE B AACH, ALBERT C AACHEN, HENRY D

12. BILLHARDT, PHILIP 12.____
A BILLERA, FRANKLIN B BILLIG, LESLIE C BILLINGS, CAROL D

13. LADEROS, ELANA 13.____
A LADENHEIM, HELENE B LADERMAN, SAM C LADHA, SANDRA D

14. PUCKERING, DENNIS 14.____
A PUCKETT, AUDREY B PUCKNAT, JOHN C PUCKO, BENNY D

15. SCHOLZE, GEORGE 15.____
A SCHOLNICK, LEONARD B SCHOLOSS, JACK C SCHOLZ, PAUL D

16. WILSON, MERYL 16.____
A WILSON, MERIMAN B WILSON, MERRY C WILSON, MERRYL D

17. ZUKOWSKI, MICHAEL 17.____
A ZWACK, ALEXA B ZYKO, KATHERINE C ZYMAN, HERBERT D

18. MC CANNA, THOMAS 18.____
A MC CANN, GERALD B MC CANNA, JANET C MC CANTS, MOLLIE D

19. PHILIPP, SUSANE 19.____
A PHILIP, PETER B PHILIPOSE, ANDREW C PHILIPPE, BEATRICE D

20. KINGPIN, PAUL 20.____
A KINGDON, KENNETH B KINGMAN, JEAN C KINGOLD, RICHARD D

21. HAMILTON, DONALD 21.____
A HAMILTON, DON B HAMILTON, DOROTHY C HAMILTON, DOUGLAS D

22. BAEL, ELAINE 22.____
A BAELE, GUSTAVE B BAEN, JAMES C BAENA, ARIEL D

23. BILL, KASEY 23.____
A BILGINER, NATHAN B BILKAY, WILLIAM C BILLES, BRADFORD D

24. CARLEN, ELLIOT 24.____
A CARINO, NAN B CARLE, JOHN C CARLESI, ANTHONY D

25. LOURIE, DONALD 25.____
A LOUIE, ROSE B LOUIS, STEVE C LOVE, MARCIA D

KEY (CORRECT ANSWERS)

1. B
2. A
3. C
4. B
5. C

6. D
7. C
8. D
9. A
10. B

11. A
12. B
13. C
14. A
15. D

16. D
17. A
18. C
19. C
20. D

21. B
22. A
23. C
24. C
25. C

TEST 4

DIRECTIONS: For each of the following, you are given a name above and three other names in alphabetical order below. The letters A, B, C, and D stand for spaces where you could file the name. Find the CORRECT space for the name given above so that it will be in alphabetical order with the names below it. The letter that stands for that space is the answer to the question.

1. DEMOPOULOS, GUS 1.____
A DEMOPOULOS, DIMITRI B DEMOPOULOS, HELEN C DEMOPOULOS, LAURA D

2. DRUMWRIGHT, BRUCE 2.____
A DRUMMOND, RANDY B DRUMMUND, WALTER C DRUMRIGHT, JULIUS D

3. GRAHAM, LETICIA 3.____
A GRAHAM, LEON B GRAHAM, LEROY C GRAHAM, LESLIE D

4. KELLEHER, KEVIN 4.____
A KELLARD, WILLIAM B KELLEDY, JAMES C KELLEHER, KRISTINE D

5. LIANG, JAN 5.____
A LIANG, JIE B LIANG, JIN CHANG C LIANG, JIN HE D

6. MOLINELLI, STEVE 6.____
A MOLINAR, RICARDO B MOLINER, LOUISA C MOLINI, OSCAR D

7. PARRILLA, EMANUEL 7.____
A PARRAS, TONY B PARRETTA, JOSEPHINE C PARRETTA, NANCY D

8. SILBERFARD, MILDRED 8.____
A SILBERBERG, SEYMOUR B SILBERBLATT, JOHN C SILBERFARB, SYLVIA D

9. TOLANI, ROHET 9.____
A TOLAN, DOROTHY B TOLASSI, JOANNA C TOLBERT, ALICE D

10. VIERA, DIANE 10.____
A VIERA, DIANA B VIERA, ELLIOT C VIERA, JAMES D

11. KLAUER, MICHAEL 11.____
A KLAUBER, ALFRED B KLAUBERG, SUSAN C KLAUS, MARJORIE D

12. REEVES, MARIE 12.____
A REEVES, MATTHEW B REEVES, MELVIN C REEVES, ORALEE D

13. DEL VALLE, JULIA 13.____
A DEL VALLE, EMMA B DEL VALLE, GLORIA C DEL VALLE, JOSEPH D

14. LAIO, SHU-YU 14.____
A LAING, VINCENT B LAIRO, SCOTT C LAIS, STEVE D

15. MENDEZ, ROBERTO 15.____
A MENDELSON, SOL B MENDES, MAE C MENDOZA, HUGO D

16. ALBRIGHT, LEE 16.____
A ALBRACHT, MARIE B ALBRECHT, VICTOR C ALBRINK, JOAN D

17. CAIN, STEPHEN 17.____
A CAIN, SAMUEL B CAIN, SHARON C CAIN, SIBOL D

18. HOPKOWITZ, THOMAS 18.____
A HOPKINS, CYNTHIA B HOPPENFELD, DENIS C HOPPER, ELSA D

19. LUMBLY, KAREN 19.____
A LUMBI, JENNY B LUME, JIMMIE C LUMEN, GAIL D

20. MAYER, MORTON 20.____
A MAYER, MONROE B MAYER, MORRIS C MAYER, MYRON D

21. YOUNGER, LORRAINE 21.____
A YOUNGHEM, THEODORE B YOUNGMAN, LEIF C YOUNGS, FRED D

22. THORSEN, HILDA 22.____
A THORNWELL, PERCY B THORON, LLOYD C THORP, JACQUELINE D

23. MC DERMOTT, BETTY 23.____
A MC DEARMON, WILLIAM B MC DEVITT, BERYL C MC DONAGH, DANIEL D

24. BLUMENTHAL, SIMON 24.____
A BLUMENTHAL, SHIRLEY B BLUMENTHAL, SIDNEY C BLUMENTHAL, SOLOMON D

25. ERVINS, RICHARD 25.____
A ERVIN, BERTHA B ERVING, THELMA C ERWIN, EUGENE D

KEY (CORRECT ANSWERS)

1. B
2. D
3. D
4. C
5. A
6. B
7. D
8. D
9. B
10. B
11. C
12. A
13. D
14. B
15. C
16. C
17. D
18. B
19. B
20. C
21. A
22. D
23. B
24. C
25. C

TEST 5

DIRECTIONS: For each of the following, you are given a name above and three other names in alphabetical order below. The letters A, B, C, and D stand for spaces where you could file the name. Find the CORRECT space for the name given above so that it will be in alphabetical order with the names below it. The letter that stands for that space is the answer to the question.

1. GUIDRY, THELMA 1.____
A GUIDONE, GEORGE B GUIGLI, PAMELA C GUIGNON, DANIEL D

2. JAMES, ALLAN 2.____
A JAMES, ALMA B JAMES, AMY C JAMES, ANNA D

3. LESSOFF, CONNIE 3.____
A LESSIK, JAKE B LESSING, LEONARD C LESSNER, ADELE D

4. MONTNER, LUIS 4.____
A MONTEFIORE, ANDREW B MONTILLA, IRIS C MONTINI, ALEXANDRA D

5. PHELPS, KENNETH 5.____
A PHELEN, JAMES B PHELON, RANDY C PHETT, GARY D

6. STAVSKY, STANLEY 6.____
A STAVROS, MIKE B STAWSKI, LILLIAN C STAWSKI, NAOMI D

7. GROSSMAN, WILL 7.____
A GROSSMAN, WENDY B GROSSMANN, WAYNE C GROSSMANN, WILLA D

8. IRES, JEFFREY 8.____
A IRENA, THOMAS B IRENE, JAY C IRES, HOWARD D

9. NIKOLAOU, CHRISTINE 9.____
A NIKOLAIS, GERRARD B NIKOLAKAKOS, GEORGE C NIKOLATOS, HARRY D

10. TURCO, KEITH 10.____
A TURCHIN, DEBORAH B TURCI, GINA C TURCK, KATHRYN D

11. WORLEY, DIANE 11.____
A WORMAN, STELLA B WORMER, SARA C WORMLEY, ROBERT D

12. DRUSIN, GUY 12.____
A DRURY, JESSICA B DRUSE, KEN C DRUSS, THERESA D

13. LYONS, JAMES 13.____
A LYONS, ERNST B LYONS, INGRID C LYONS, KEVIN D

14. NOBLE, BERNARD 14.____
A NOBEL, LOUISE B NOBILE, DENNIS C NOBIS, JAMES D

15. O'DELL, ERIN 15.____
A O'DAY, PATRICIA B O'DEA, MAUREEN C O'DELL, GWYNN D

16. POUPON, LOUIS 16.____
A POULSON, SIMON B POURE, DAMIAN C POURIDAS, CARMEN D

17. REMEY, NAOMI 17.____
A REMES, STUART B REMEZ, ALFREDO C REMIEN, ROBERT D

18. WATSON, LAURENCE 18.____
A WATSON, LENORA B WATSON, LEONARD C WATSON, LLOYD D

19. AMSILI, MORTON 19.____
A AMSDEN, ESTHER B AMSEL, HYMAN C ARES, MEYER D

20. CLEMMONS, BERTHA 20.____
A CLEMENT, GILBERT B CLEMINSON, DEAN C CLEMONS, GLADYS D

21. LAMPERT, EDNA 21.____
A LAMPIER, JANICE B LAMPKIN, ALYCE C LAMPKOWSKI, DENNIS D

22. LIBERTO, DON 22.____
A LIBERMAN, MATTIE B LIBERSON, MIRIAM C LIBERTY, ARTHUR D

23. REVENZON, ISABELLA 23.____
A REVELEY, RUTH B REVELLE, GRACE C REVERE, EDITH D

24. BURKHALTER, HAZEL 24.____
A BURKE, WINSTON B BURKETT, BENJAMIN C BURKEY, WAYNE D

25. DORSEY, HAROLD 25.____
A DOSHER, EILEEN B DOSHIRE, BURTON C DOSSIL, RICHARD D

KEY (CORRECT ANSWERS)

1. B
2. A
3. D
4. D
5. C

6. B
7. B
8. D
9. C
10. D

11. A
12. C
13. C
14. D
15. C

16. B
17. B
18. A
19. C
20. C

21. A
22. C
23. C
24. D
25. A

TEST 6

DIRECTIONS: For each of the following, you are given a name above and three other names in alphabetical order below. The letters A, B, C, and D stand for spaces where you could file the name. Find the CORRECT space for the name given above so that it will be in alphabetical order with the names below it. The letter that stands for that space is the answer to the question.

1. HATFIELD, NICOLA 1.____
A HATCHER, JOHN B HATELY, BRIAN C HATGIS, ELLEN D

2. IVANOFF, HELENA 2.____
A IVAN, LEONARD B IVANOV, SERGE C IVANY, EMERY D

3. KELKER, NORMAN 3.____
A KELFER, STEPHANE B KELING, JAY C KELISON, ABE D

4. ROGGENBURG, LEE 4.____
A ROGERS, SHARON B ROGET, ALLAN C ROGGERO, MORGAN D

5. SMITH, ALENA 5.____
A SMITH, AARON B SMITH, AGNES C SMITH, ALBERT D

6. ZOLOR, RONALD 6.____
A ZOLNAK, SUSANNA B ZOLOTH, SAMUEL C ZOLOTO, PEARL D

7. ERRICH, GRETCHEN 7.____
A ERREICH, RENE B ERRERA, STEVEN C ERRETT, ALICE D

8. CARDWELL, MELASAN 8.____
A CARDUCCI, RONALD B CARDULLO, MIKE C CARDY, FREDRIK D

9. MOFFAT, SARAH 9.____
A MOFFET, JONATHAN B MOFFIE, LISA C MOFFITT, LAUREN D

10. PARRINO, WAYNE 10.____
A PARRETTA, MICHELE B PARRILLA, BERNIE C PARRINELLO, CARRIE D

11. PINSLEY, SETH 11.____
A PINSKY, GLORIA B PINSON, BENNET C PINTADO, MARIE D

12. FREEMAN, ELMIRA 12.____
A FREEMAN, EDITH B FREEMAN, ERIC C FREEMAN, ETHEL D

13. BERLINGER, SOPHIE 13.____
A BERLEY, DAVID B BERLIND, ARNOLD C BERLINGER, FREDA D

14. ANIELLO, JOSEPH 14.____
A ANGULO, ADOLFO B ANHALT, LINDA C ANIBAL, VINCENT D

15. LACHER, LEO 15.____
A LACHET, MARGARET B LACHINI, KAY C LACHIVER, ANDREA D

16. ROBINSON, MARION 16.___
A ROBINSON, MARCIA B ROBINSON, MARGARET C ROBINSON, MARIETTA D

17. ULRICH, DENNIS 17.___
A ULMAN, CANDY B ULMER, TED C ULRIED, RICHARD D

18. ASHINSKY, ROSS 18.___
A ASHKAR, MICHAEL B ASHKE, PAUL C ASHKIN, ROBERTA D

19. LITVAK, DARRELL 19.___
A LITUCHY, BEVERLY B LITVIN, SAM C LITWACK, MARTIN D

20. SLATTERY, GERALD 20.___
A SLATER, NELLIE B SLATKIN, HEIDI C SLATKY, IRVING D

21. MCCANTS, GEORGIA 21.___
A MCCANN, CHERYL B MCCANNA, THOMAS C MCCARDELL, GARY D

22. HARMER, AVA 22.___
A HARLOW, JULES B HARLSON, NORMAN C HARMEL, SHARON D

23. CALDERONE, PHILIP 23.___
A CALDERIN, ANA B CALDON, WALTER C CALDRON, MICHELE D

24. GINSBURG, ISAAC 24.___
A GINSBURG, EDWARD B GINSBURG, GERALD C GINSBURG, HILDA D

25. LEE, LEIGH 25.___
A LEE, LELA B LEE, LELAND C LEE, LEON D

KEY (CORRECT ANSWERS)

1. C
2. B
3. D
4. C
5. D

6. B
7. D
8. C
9. A
10. D

11. B
12. B
13. D
14. D
15. A

16. D
17. C
18. A
19. B
20. D

21. C
22. D
23. B
24. D
25. A

TEST 7

DIRECTIONS: For each of the following, you are given a name above and three other names in alphabetical order below. The letters A, B, C, and D stand for spaces where you could file the name. Find the CORRECT space for the name given above so that it will be in alphabetical order with the names below it. The letter that stands for that space is the answer to the question.

1. POWERS, PHYLLIS 1.____
A POWELL, HATTIE B POWER, EDWARD C POWLETT, WENDY D

2. SILVERA, IRWIN 2.____
A SILVA, ANGEL B SILVANO, FRANK C SILVERIA, ANNA D

3. BACHRACH, DAN 3.____
A BACHMANN, DONNA B BACHNER, LESTER C BACHOWSKI, JEWEL D

4. RIVERA, RAMON 4.____
A RIVAS, ERICA B RIVES, SHARON C RIVIER, CLAUDE D

5. WEINSTOCK, JEFFREY 5.____
A WEINSTEIN, PAUL B WEINSTONE, ALAN C WEINTRAUB, MARCI D

6. AMANDA, STEPHAN 6.____
A AMADO, DANIELLO B AMALIA, JOSE C AMAR, LISA D

7. HERRON, LOUIS 7.____
A HERSCH, JACK B HERSCHELL, GREGORY C HERSCHER, GAIL D

8. REEDY, ARTHUR 8.____
A REED, ALEX B REESE, JOHN C REEVE, DAVE D

9. FLORIN, RAYMOND 9.____
A FLORENTINO, PAULA B FLORES, MITCHEL C FLORIAN, CARLO D

10. HOROWITZ, ELLIOT 10.____
A HOROWITZ, FRANKLIN B HOROWITZ, IRA C HOROWITZ, JOAN D

11. KNOPFLER, WOODY 11.____
A KNOBLER, HENRY B KNOLL, GEORGE C KNOPF, LAURA D

12. OTIN, JENNIFER 12.____
A OTERO, ALBERT B OTHON, DOROTHY C OTIS, JAMES D

13. SACHA, IRENE 13.____
A SACCO, HEATHER B SACHNER, JULIE C SACHS, DAVID D

14. WORTHY, PRISCILLA 14.____
A WORTH, ROBERT B WORTHINGTON, SUSAN C WORTMAN, MYRA D

15. ZUCKERMAN, GARY 15.____
A ZUKER, JEROME B ZUKOWSKI, CHRIS C ZULACK, JOHN D

16. BRIEGER, CLARENCE 16.____
A BRIEF, SIGMUND B BRIELLE, JEAN C BRIELOFF, SAUL D

17. FOSTER, AGNES 17.____
A FOSTER, ADDIE B FOSTER, ALBERT C FOSTER, ALICE D

18. LIBERSTEIN, MIRIAM 18.____
A LIBERMAN, HERMAN B LIBERSON, RUBIN C LIBERT, NAT D

19. PRICKETT, DELORES 19.____
A PRICE, WILLIAM B PRICHARD, STEPHANY C PRITCHETT, KENNETH D

20. TRIBBLE, RITA 20.____
A TRIAS, JOSE B TRIBBIT, CHARLES C TRIBE, SIENNA D

21. ZOBEL, MAX 21.____
A ZOBACK, DERRICK B ZOBALI, KIERSTAN C ZOBERG, STUART D

22. HOTRA, WALTER 22.____
A HOTT, NELL B HOTTENSEN, ROBERT C HOTTON, BRUCE D

23. MICHELL, CARL 23.____
A MICHELE, KAREN B MICHELMAN, BERTHA C MICHELS, GLORIA D

24. RAFFERTY, GEORGE 24.____
A RAFFERTY, HAROLD B RAFFERTY, KEVIN C RAFFERTY, LUCILLE D

25. OLIVIERI, ALLAN 25.____
A OLIVIERO, FRANK B OLIVRY, RAUL C OLIZEIRA, CHARLES D

KEY (CORRECT ANSWERS)

1. C
2. C
3. D
4. B
5. B
6. C
7. A
8. B
9. D
10. A
11. D
12. C
13. B
14. C
15. A
16. B
17. B
18. C
19. C
20. C
21. C
22. A
23. B
24. A
25. A

SPELLING
EXAMINATION SECTION
TEST 1

DIRECTIONS: Each question or incomplete statement is followed by several suggested answers or completions. Select the one that BEST answers the question or completes the statement. *PRINT THE LETTER OF THE CORRECT ANSWER IN THE SPACE AT THE RIGHT.*

Questions 1-5.

DIRECTIONS: Questions 1 through 5 consist of four words. Indicate the letter of the word that is CORRECTLY spelled.

1. A. harassment B. harrasment C. harasment D. harrassment 1.____

2. A. maintainance B. maintenence C. maintainence D. maintenance 2.____

3. A. comparable B. comprable C. comparible D. commparable 3.____

4. A. suficient B. sufficiant C. sufficient D. suficiant 4.____

5. A. fairly B. fairley C. farely D. fairlie 5.____

Questions 6-10.

DIRECTIONS: Questions 6 through 10 consist of four words. Indicate the letter of the word that is INCORRECTLY spelled.

6. A. pallor B. ballid C. ballet D. pallid 6.____

7. A. urbane B. surburbane C. interurban D. urban

8. A. facial B. physical C. fiscle D. muscle 8.____

9. A. interceed B. benefited C. analogous D. altogether

10. A. seizure B. irrelevant C. inordinate D. dissapproved

KEY (CORRECT ANSWERS)

1.	A	6.	B
2.	D	7.	B
3.	A	8.	C
4.	C	9.	A
5.	A	10.	D

TEST 2

DIRECTIONS: Each of Questions 1 through 15 consists of two words preceded by the letters A and B. In each question, one of the words may be spelled INCORRECTLY or both words may be spelled CORRECTLY. If one of the words in a question is spelled INCORRECTLY, print in the space at the right the capital letter preceding the INCORRECTLY spelled word. If both words are spelled CORRECTLY, print the letter C.

1. A. easely B. readily 1.____
2. A. pursue B. decend 2.____
3. A. measure B. laboratory 3.____
4. A. exausted B. traffic 4.____
5. A. discussion B. unpleasant 5.____
6. A. campaign B. murmer 6.____
7. A. guarantee B. sanatary 7.____
8. A. communication B. safty 8.____
9. A. numerus B. celebration 9.____
10. A. nourish B. begining 10.____
11. A. courious B. witness 11.____
12. A. undoubtedly B. thoroughly 12.____
13. A. accessible B. artifical 13.____
14. A. feild B. arranged 14.____
15. A. admittence B. hastily 15.____

KEY (CORRECT ANSWERS)

1.	A	6.	B	11.	A
2.	B	7.	B	12.	C
3.	C	8.	B	13.	B
4.	A	9.	A	14.	A
5.	C	10.	B	15.	A

TEST 3

DIRECTIONS: In each of the following sentences, one word is misspelled. Following each sentence is a list of four words taken from the sentence. Indicate the letter of the word which is MISSPELLED in the sentence. *PRINT THE LETTER OF THE CORRECT ANSWER IN THE SPACE AT THE RIGHT.*

1. The placing of any inflammable substance in any building, or the placing of any device or contrivence capable of producing fire, for the purpose of causing a fire is an attempt to burn. 1.____

   A. inflammable B. substance
   C. device D. contrivence

2. The word *break* also means obtaining an entrance into a building by any artifice used for that purpose, or by colussion with any person therein. 2.____

   A. obtaining B. entrance
   C. artifice D. colussion

3. Any person who with intent to provoke a breech of the peace causes a disturbance or is offensive to others may be deemed to have committed disorderly conduct. 3.____

   A. breech B. disturbance
   C. offensive D. committed

4. When the offender inflicts a grevious harm upon the person from whose possession, or in whose presence, property is taken, he is guilty of robbery. 4.____

   A. offender B. grevious
   C. possession D. presence

5. A person who wilfuly encourages or advises another person in attempting to take the latter's life is guilty of a felony. 5.____

   A. wilfuly B. encourages
   C. advises D. attempting

6. He maliciously demurred to an ajournment of the proceedings. 6.____

   A. maliciously B. demurred
   C. ajournment D. proceedings

7. His innocence at that time is irrelevant in view of his more recent villianous demeanor. 7.____

   A. innocence B. irrelevant
   C. villianous D. demeanor

8. The mischievous boys aggrevated the annoyance of their neighbor. 8.____

   A. mischievous B. aggrevated
   C. annoyance D. neighbor

9. While his perseverence was commendable, his judgment was debatable. 9.____

   A. perseverence B. commendable
   C. judgment D. debatable

10. He was hoping the appeal would facilitate his aquittal. 10.___

A. hoping
B. appeal
C. facilitate
D. aquittal

11. It would be preferable for them to persue separate courses. 11.___

A. preferable
B. persue
C. separate
D. courses

12. The litigant was complimented on his persistance and achievement. 12.___

A. litigant
B. complimented
C. persistance
D. achievement

13. Ocassionally there are discrepancies in the descriptions of miscellaneous items. 13.___

A. ocassionally
B. discrepancies
C. descriptions
D. miscellaneous

14. The councilmanic seargent-at-arms enforced the prohibition. 14.___

A. councilmanic
B. seargent-at-arms
C. enforced
D. prohibition

15. The teacher had an ingenious device for maintaning attendance. 15.___

A. ingenious
B. device
C. maintaning
D. attendance

16. A worrysome situation has developed as a result of the assessment that absenteeism is increasing despite our conscientious efforts. 16.___

A. worrysome
B. assessment
C. absenteeism
D. conscientious

17. I concurred with the credit manager that it was practicable to charge purchases on a biennial basis, and the company agreed to adhear to this policy. 17.___

A. concurred
B. practicable
C. biennial
D. adhear

18. The pastor was chagrined and embarassed by the irreverent conduct of one of his parishioners. 18.___

A. chagrined
B. embarassed
C. irreverent
D. parishioners

19. His inate seriousness was belied by his flippant demeanor. 19.___

A. inate
B. belied
C. flippant
D. demeanor

20. It was exceedingly regrettable that the excessive number of challanges in the court delayed the start of the trial. 20.___

A. exceedingly
B. regrettable
C. excessive
D. challanges

KEY (CORRECT ANSWERS)

1. D
2. D
3. A
4. B
5. A
6. C
7. C
8. B
9. A
10. D
11. B
12. C
13. A
14. B
15. C
16. A
17. D
18. B
19. A
20. D

TEST 4

Questions 1-11.

DIRECTIONS: Each question consists of three words. In each question, one of the words may be spelled incorrectly or all three may be spelled correctly. For each question. if one of the words is spelled INCORRECTLY, write the letter of the incorrect word in the space at the right. If all three words are spelled CORRECTLY, write the letter D in the space at the right.

SAMPLE I: (A) guide (B) department (C) stranger
SAMPLE II: (A) comply (B) valuable (C) window
In Sample I, departmint is incorrect. It should be spelled department. Therefore, B is the answer.
In Sample II, all three words are spelled correctly. Therefore, D is the answer.

1.	A. argument	B. reciept	C. complain	1.__
2.	A. sufficient	B. postpone	C. visible	2.__
3.	A. expirience	B. dissatisfy	C. alternate	3.__
4.	A. occurred	B. noticable	C. appendix	4.__
5.	A. anxious	B. guarantee	C. calender	5.__
6.	A. sincerely	B. affectionately	C. truly	6.__
7.	A. excellant	B. verify	C. important	7.__
8.	A. error	B. quality	C. enviroment	8.__
9.	A. exercise	B. advance	C. pressure	9.__
10.	A. citizen	B. expence	C. memory	10.__
11.	A. flexable	B. focus	C. forward	11.__

Questions 12-15.

DIRECTIONS: Each of Questions 12 through 15 consists of a group of four words. Examine each group carefully; then in the space at the right, indicate
A - if only one word in the group is spelled correctly
B - if two words in the group are spelled correctly
C - if three words in the group are spelled correctly
D - if all four words in the group are spelled correctly

12. Wendsday, particular, similar, hunderd 12.__

13. realize, judgment, opportunities, consistent 13.__

14. equel, principle, assistense, commitee 14.__

15. simultaneous, privilege, advise, ocassionaly 15.__

KEY (CORRECT ANSWERS)

1. B
2. D
3. A
4. B
5. C
6. D
7. A
8. C
9. D
10. B
11. A
12. B
13. D
14. A
15. C

TEST 5

DIRECTIONS: Each of Questions 1 through 15 consists of two words preceded by the letters A and B. In each item, one of the words may be spelled INCORRECTLY or both words may be spelled CORRECTLY. If one of the words in a question is spelled INCORRECTLY, print in the space at the right the letter preceding the INCORRECTLY spelled word. If both words are spelled CORRECTLY, print the letter C.

1. A. justified B. offering 1.___
2. A. predjudice B. license 2.___
3. A. label B. pamphlet 3.___
4. A. bulletin B. physical 4.___
5. A. assure B. exceed 5.___
6. A. advantagous B. evident 6.___
7. A. benefit B. occured 7.___
8. A. acquire B. graditude 8.___
9. A. amenable B. boundry 9.___
10. A. deceive B. voluntary 10.___
11. A. imunity B. conciliate 11.___
12. A. acknoledge B. presume 12.___
13. A. substitute B. prespiration 13.___
14. A. reputible B. announce 14.___
15. A. luncheon B. wretched 15.___

KEY (CORRECT ANSWERS)

1. C	6. A	11. A
2. A	7. B	12. A
3. C	8. B	13. B
4. C	9. B	14. A
5. C	10. C	15. C

TEST 6

DIRECTIONS: Questions 1 through 15 contain lists of words, one of which is misspelled. Indicate the MISSPELLED word in each group. *PRINT THE LETTER OF THE CORRECT ANSWER IN THE SPACE AT THE RIGHT.*

1. A. felony B. lacerate C. cancellation D. seperate

2. A. batallion B. beneficial C. miscellaneous D. secretary

3. A. camouflage B. changeable C. embarass D. inoculate 3.____

4. A. beneficial B. disasterous C. incredible D. miniature

5. A. auxilliary B. hypocrisy C. phlegm D. vengeance 5.____

6. A. aisle B. cemetary C. courtesy D. extraordinary

7. A. crystallize B. innoculate C. eminent D. symmetrical

8. A. judgment B. maintainance C. bouillon D. eery

9. A. isosceles B. ukulele C. mayonaise D. iridescent 9.____

10. A. remembrance B. occurence C. correspondence D. countenance

11. A. corpuscles B. mischievous C. batchelor D. bulletin

12. A. terrace B. banister C. concrete D. masonery 12.____

13. A. balluster B. gutter C. latch D. bridging 13.____

14. A. personnell B. navel C. therefor D. emigrant 14.____

15. A. committee B. submiting C. amendment D. electorate 15.____

KEY (CORRECT ANSWERS)

1.	D	6.	B	11.	C
2.	A	7.	B	12.	D
3.	C	8.	B	13.	A
4.	B	9.	C	14.	A
5.	A	10.	B	15.	B

TEST 7

Questions 1-5.

DIRECTIONS: Questions 1 through 5 consist of groups of four words. Select answer:
A if only ONE word is spelled correctly in a group
B if TWO words are spelled correctly in a group
C if THREE words are spelled correctly in a group
D if all FOUR words are spelled correctly in a group

1. counterfeit, embarass, panicky, supercede 1.___

2. benefited, personnel, questionnaire, unparalelled 2.___

3. bankruptcy describable, proceed, vacuum 3.___

4. handicapped, mispell, offerred, pilgrimmage 4.___

5. corduroy, interfere, privilege, separator 5.___

Questions 6-10.

DIRECTIONS: Questions 6 through 10 consist of four pairs of words each. Some of the words are spelled correctly; others are spelled incorrectly. For each question, indicate in the space at the right the letter preceding that pair of words in which BOTH words are spelled CORRECTLY.

6. A. hygienic, inviegle B. omniscience, pittance 6.___
C. plagarize, nullify D. seargent, perilous

7. A. auxilary, existence B. pronounciation, accordance 7.___
C. ignominy, indegence D. suable, baccalaureate

8. A. discreet, inaudible B. hypocrisy, currupt 8.___
C. liquidate, maintainance D. transparancy, onerous

9. A. facility, stimulent B. frugel, sanitary 9.___
C. monetary, prefatory D. punctileous, credentials

10. A. bankruptsy, perceptible B. disuade, resilient 10.___
C. exhilerate, expectancy D. panegyric, disparate

Questions 11-15

DIRECTIONS: Each question or incomplete statement is followed by several suggested answers or completions. Select the one that BEST answers the question or completes the statement. *PRINT THE LETTER OF THE CORRECT ANSWER IN THE SPACE AT THE RIGHT.*

11. The silent *e* must be retained when the suffix *-able* is added to the word 11.___

A. argue B. love C. move D. notice

12. The CORRECTLY spelled word in the choices below is 12.___

A. kindergarden B. zylophone
C. hemorrhage D. mayonaise

13. Of the following words, the one spelled CORRECTLY is 13.____

A. begger B. cemetary
C. embarassed D. coyote

14. Of the following words, the one spelled CORRECTLY is 14.____

A. dandilion B. wiry C. sieze D. rythmic

15. Of the following words, the one spelled CORRECTLY is 15.____

A. beligerent B. anihilation
C. facetious D. adversery

KEY (CORRECT ANSWERS)

1.	B	6.	B	11.	D
2.	C	7.	D	12.	C
3.	D	8.	A	13.	D
4.	A	9.	C	14.	B
5.	D	10.	D	15.	C

TEST 8

DIRECTIONS: In each of the following sentences, one word is misspelled. Following each sentence is a list of four words taken from the sentence. Indicate the letter of the word which is MISSPELLED. *PRINT THE LETTER OF THE CORRECT ANSWER IN THE SPACE AT THE RIGHT.*

1. If the administrator attempts to withold information, there is a good likelihood that there will be serious repercussions. 1.___

   A. administrator B. withold
   C. likelihood D. repercussions

2. He condescended to apologize, but we felt that a beligerent person should not occupy an influential position. 2.___

   A. condescended B. apologize
   C. beligerent D. influential

3. Despite the sporadic delinquent payments of his indebtedness, Mr. Johnson has been an exemplery customer. 3.___

   A. sporadic B. delinquent
   C. indebtedness D. exemplery

4. He was appreciative of the support he consistantly acquired, but he felt that he had waited an inordinate length of time for it. 4.___

   A. appreciative B. consistantly
   C. acquired D. inordinate

5. Undeniably they benefited from the establishment of a receivership, but the question of statutary limitations remained unresolved. 5.___

   A. undeniably B. benefited
   C. receivership D. statutary

6. Mr. Smith profered his hand as an indication that he considered it a viable contract, but Mr. Nelson alluded to the fact that his colleagues had not been consulted. 6.___

   A. profered B. viable
   C. alluded D. colleagues

7. The treatments were beneficial according to the optometrists, and the consensus was that minimal improvement could be expected. 7.___

   A. beneficial B. optomotrists
   C. consensus D. minimal

8. Her frivalous manner was unbecoming because the air of solemnity at the cemetery was pervasive. 8.___

   A. frivalous B. solemnity
   C. cemetery D. pervasive

9. The clandestine meetings were designed to make the two adversaries more amicable, but they served only to intensify their emnity. 9.___

   A. clandestine B. adversaries
   C. amicable D. emnity

10. Do you think that his innovative ideas and financial acumen will help stabalize the fluctuations of the stock market? 10.____

A. innovative
B. acumen
C. stabalize
D. fluctuations

11. In order to keep a perpetual inventory, you will have to keep an uninterrupted surveillance of all the miscellanious stock. 11.____

A. perpetual
B. uninterrupted
C. surveillance
D. miscellanious

12. She used the art of pursuasion on the children because she found that caustic remarks had no perceptible effect on their behavior. 12.____

A. pursuasion
B. caustic
C. perceptible
D. effect

13. His sacreligious outbursts offended his constituents, and he was summarily removed from office by the City Council. 13.____

A. sacreligious
B. constituents
C. summarily
D. Council

14. They exhorted the contestants to greater efforts, but the exhorbitant costs in terms of energy expended resulted in a feeling of lethargy. 14.____

A. exhorted
B. contestants
C. exhorbitant
D. lethargy

15. Since he was knowledgable about illicit drugs, he was served with a subpoena to appear for the prosecution. 15.____

A. knowledgable
B. illicit
C. subpoena
D. prosecution

16. In spite of his lucid statements, they denigrated his report and decided it should be succintly paraphrased. 16.____

A. lucid
B. denigrated
C. succintly
D. paraphrased

17. The discussion was not germane to the contraversy, but the indicted man's insistence on further talk was allowed. 17.____

A. germane
B. contraversy
C. indicted
D. insistence

18. The legislators were enervated by the distances they had traveled during the election year to fullfil their speaking engagements. 18.____

A. legislators
B. enervated
C. traveled
D. fullfil

19. The plaintiffs' attornies charged the defendant in the case with felonious assault. 19.___

A. plaintiffs'
B. attornies
C. defendant
D. felonious

20. It is symptomatic of the times that we try to placate all, but a proposal for new forms of disciplinery action was promulgated by the staff. 20.___

A. symptomatic
B. placate
C. disciplinery
D. promulgated

KEY (CORRECT ANSWERS)

1.	B	6.	A	11.	D	16.	C
2.	C	7.	B	12.	A	17.	B
3.	D	8.	A	13.	A	18.	D
4.	B	9.	D	14.	C	19.	B
5.	D	10.	C	15.	A	20.	C

TEST 9

DIRECTIONS: Each of Questions 1 through 15 consists of a single word which is spelled either correctly or incorrectly. If the word is spelled CORRECTLY, you are to print the letter C (Correct) in the space at the right. If the word is spelled INCORRECTLY, you are to print the letter W (Wrong).

1. pospone 1.____
2. diffrent 2.____
3. height 3.____
4. carefully 4.____
5. ability 5.____
6. temper 6.____
7. deslike 7.____
8. seldem 8.____
9. alcohol 9.____
10. expense 10.____
11. vegatable 11.____
12. dispensary 12.____
13. specemin 13.____
14. allowance 14.____
15. exersise 15.____

KEY (CORRECT ANSWERS)

1.	W	6.	C	11.	W
2.	W	7.	W	12.	C
3.	C	8.	W	13.	W
4.	C	9.	C	14.	C
5.	C	10.	C	15.	W

TEST 10

DIRECTIONS: Each of Questions 1 through 10 consists of four words, one of which may be spelled incorrectly or all four words may be spelled correctly. If one of the words in a question is spelled incorrectly, print in the space at the right the capital letter preceding the word which is spelled INCORRECTLY. If all four words are spelled CORRECTLY, print the letter E.

1.	A. dismissal	B. collateral	C. leisure	D. proffession	1.___
2.	A. subsidary	B. outrageous	C. liaison	D. assessed	2.___
3.	A. already	B. changeable	C. mischevous	D. cylinder	3.___
4.	A. supersede	B. deceit	C. dissension	D. imminent	4.___
5.	A. arguing	B. contagious	C. comparitive	D. accessible	5.___
6.	A. indelible	B. existance	C. presumptuous	D. mileage	6.___
7.	A. extention	B. aggregate	C. sustenance	D. gratuitous	7.___
8.	A. interrogate	B. exaggeration	C. vacillate	D. moreover	8.___
9.	A. parallel	B. derogatory	C. admissable	D. appellate	9.___
10.	A. safety	B. cumalative	C. disappear	D. usable	10.___

KEY (CORRECT ANSWERS)

1. D	6. B
2. A	7. A
3. C	8. E
4. E	9. C
5. C	10. B

TEST 11

DIRECTIONS: Each of Questions 1 through 10 consists of four words, one of which may be spelled incorrectly or all four words may be spelled correctly. If one of the words in a question is spelled INCORRECTLY, print in the space at the right the capital letter preceding the word which is spelled incorrectly. If all four words are spelled CORRECTLY, print the letter E.

1. A. vehicular B. gesticulate C. manageable D. fullfil 1.____

2. A. inovation B. onerous C. chastise D. irresistible 2.____

3. A. familiarize B. dissolution C. oscillate D. superflous 3.____

4. A. census B. defender C. adherence D. inconceivable 4.____

5. A. voluminous B. liberalize C. bankrupcy D. conversion 5.____

6. A. justifiable B. executor C. perpatrate D. dispelled 6.____

7. A. boycott B. abeyence C. enterprise D. circular 7.____

8. A. spontaineous B. dubious C. analyze D. premonition 8.____

9. A. intelligible B. apparently C. genuine D. crucial 9.____

10. A. plentiful B. ascertain C. carreer D. preliminary 10.____

KEY (CORRECT ANSWERS)

1. D
2. A
3. D
4. E
5. C
6. C
7. B
8. A
9. E
10. C

TEST 12

DIRECTIONS: Questions 1 through 25 consist of four words each, of which one of the words may be spelled incorrectly or all four words may be spelled correctly. If one of the words in a question is spelled INCORRECTLY, print in the space at the right the capital letter preceding the word which is spelled incorrectly. If all four words are spelled CORRECTLY, print the letter E.

1. A. temporary B. existance C. complimentary D. altogether 1._

2. A. privilege B. changeable C. jeopardize D. commitment 2._

3. A. grievous B. alloted C. outrageous D. mortgage 3._

4. A. tempermental B. accommodating C. bookkeeping D. panicky 4._

5. A. auxiliary B. indispensable C. ecstasy D. fiery 5._

6. A. dissappear B. buoyant C. imminent D. parallel 6._

7. A. loosly B. medicine C. schedule D. defendant 7._

8. A. endeavor B. persuade C. retroactive D. desparate 8._

9. A. usage B. servicable C. disadvantageous D. remittance 9._

10. A. beneficary B. receipt C. excitable D. implement 10._

11. A. accompanying B. intangible C. offerred D. movable 11._

12. A. controlling B. seize C. repetitious D. miscellaneous 12._

13. A. installation B. accommodation C. consistant D. illuminate 13._

14. A. incidentaly B. privilege C. apparent D. chargeable 14._

15. A. prevalent B. serial C. briefly D. disatisfied 15._

16. A. reciprocal B. concurrence 16.____
C. persistence D. withold

17. A. deferred B. suing 17.____
C. fulfilled D. pursuant

18. A. questionnable B. omission 18.____
C. acknowledgment D. insistent

19. A. guarantee B. committment 19.____
C. mitigate D. publicly

20. A. prerogative B. apprise 20.____
C. extrordinary D. continual

21. A. arrogant B. handicapped 21.____
C. judicious D. perennial

22. A. permissable B. deceive 22.____
C. innumerable D. retrieve

23. A. notable B. allegiance 23.____
C. reimburse D. illegal

24. A. wholly B. disbursement 24.____
C. hindrance D. conciliatory

25. A. guidance B. condemn 25.____
C. publically D. coercion

KEY (CORRECT ANSWERS)

1. B
2. E
3. B
4. A
5. E

6. A
7. A
8. D
9. B
10. A

11. C
12. E
13. C
14. A
15. D

16. D
17. E
18. A
19. B
20. C

21. E
22. A
23. E
24. E
25. C

ANSWER SHEET

EST NO. ____________ PART ______ TITLE OF POSITION ______________________________
(AS GIVEN IN EXAMINATION ANNOUNCEMENT - INCLUDE OPTION, IF ANY)

LACE OF EXAMINATION ______________________________ DATE ____________
(CITY OR TOWN) (STATE)

RATING

USE THE SPECIAL PENCIL. MAKE GLOSSY BLACK MARKS.

1 A B C D E	26 A B C D E	51 A B C D E	76 A B C D E	101 A B C D E
2 A B C D E	27 A B C D E	52 A B C D E	77 A B C D E	102 A B C D E
3 A B C D E	28 A B C D E	53 A B C D E	78 A B C D E	103 A B C D E
4 A B C D E	29 A B C D E	54 A B C D E	79 A B C D E	104 A B C D E
5 A B C D E	30 A B C D E	55 A B C D E	80 A B C D E	105 A B C D E
6 A B C D E	31 A B C D E	56 A B C D E	81 A B C D E	106 A B C D E
7 A B C D E	32 A B C D E	57 A B C D E	82 A B C D E	107 A B C D E
8 A B C D E	33 A B C D E	58 A B C D E	83 A B C D E	108 A B C D E
9 A B C D E	34 A B C D E	59 A B C D E	84 A B C D E	109 A B C D E
10 A B C D E	35 A B C D E	60 A B C D E	85 A B C D E	110 A B C D E

Make only ONE mark for each answer. Additional and stray marks may be counted as mistakes. In making corrections, erase errors COMPLETELY.

11 A B C D E	36 A B C D E	61 A B C D E	86 A B C D E	111 A B C D E
12 A B C D E	37 A B C D E	62 A B C D E	87 A B C D E	112 A B C D E
13 A B C D E	38 A B C D E	63 A B C D E	88 A B C D E	113 A B C D E
14 A B C D E	39 A B C D E	64 A B C D E	89 A B C D E	114 A B C D E
15 A B C D E	40 A B C D E	65 A B C D E	90 A B C D E	115 A B C D E
16 A B C D E	41 A B C D E	66 A B C D E	91 A B C D E	116 A B C D E
17 A B C D E	42 A B C D E	67 A B C D E	92 A B C D E	117 A B C D E
18 A B C D E	43 A B C D E	68 A B C D E	93 A B C D E	118 A B C D E
19 A B C D E	44 A B C D E	69 A B C D E	94 A B C D E	119 A B C D E
20 A B C D E	45 A B C D E	70 A B C D E	95 A B C D E	120 A B C D E
21 A B C D E	46 A B C D E	71 A B C D E	96 A B C D E	121 A B C D E
22 A B C D E	47 A B C D E	72 A B C D E	97 A B C D E	122 A B C D E
23 A B C D E	48 A B C D E	73 A B C D E	98 A B C D E	123 A B C D E
24 A B C D E	49 A B C D E	74 A B C D E	99 A B C D E	124 A B C D E
25 A B C D E	50 A B C D E	75 A B C D E	100 A B C D E	125 A B C D E

ANSWER SHEET

TEST NO. ________ PART ______ TITLE OF POSITION ____________________
(AS GIVEN IN EXAMINATION ANNOUNCEMENT - INCLUDE OPTION, IF ANY)

PLACE OF EXAMINATION ____________________ (CITY OR TOWN) ________ (STATE) DATE ________

RATING

USE THE SPECIAL PENCIL. MAKE GLOSSY BLACK MARKS.

1 A B C D E	26 A B C D E	51 A B C D E	76 A B C D E	101 A B C D E
2 A B C D E	27 A B C D E	52 A B C D E	77 A B C D E	102 A B C D E
3 A B C D E	28 A B C D E	53 A B C D E	78 A B C D E	103 A B C D E
4 A B C D E	29 A B C D E	54 A B C D E	79 A B C D E	104 A B C D E
5 A B C D E	30 A B C D E	55 A B C D E	80 A B C D E	105 A B C D E
6 A B C D E	31 A B C D E	56 A B C D E	81 A B C D E	106 A B C D E
7 A B C D E	32 A B C D E	57 A B C D E	82 A B C D E	107 A B C D E
8 A B C D E	33 A B C D E	58 A B C D E	83 A B C D E	108 A B C D E
9 A B C D E	34 A B C D E	59 A B C D E	84 A B C D E	109 A B C D E
10 A B C D E	35 A B C D E	60 A B C D E	85 A B C D E	110 A B C D E

Make only ONE mark for each answer. Additional and stray marks may be counted as mistakes. In making corrections, erase errors COMPLETELY.

11 A B C D E	36 A B C D E	61 A B C D E	86 A B C D E	111 A B C D E
12 A B C D E	37 A B C D E	62 A B C D E	87 A B C D E	112 A B C D E
13 A B C D E	38 A B C D E	63 A B C D E	88 A B C D E	113 A B C D E
14 A B C D E	39 A B C D E	64 A B C D E	89 A B C D E	114 A B C D E
15 A B C D E	40 A B C D E	65 A B C D E	90 A B C D E	115 A B C D E
16 A B C D E	41 A B C D E	66 A B C D E	91 A B C D E	116 A B C D E
17 A B C D E	42 A B C D E	67 A B C D E	92 A B C D E	117 A B C D E
18 A B C D E	43 A B C D E	68 A B C D E	93 A B C D E	118 A B C D E
19 A B C D E	44 A B C D E	69 A B C D E	94 A B C D E	119 A B C D E
20 A B C D E	45 A B C D E	70 A B C D E	95 A B C D E	120 A B C D E
21 A B C D E	46 A B C D E	71 A B C D E	96 A B C D E	121 A B C D E
22 A B C D E	47 A B C D E	72 A B C D E	97 A B C D E	122 A B C D E
23 A B C D E	48 A B C D E	73 A B C D E	98 A B C D E	123 A B C D E
24 A B C D E	49 A B C D E	74 A B C D E	99 A B C D E	124 A B C D E
25 A B C D E	50 A B C D E	75 A B C D E	100 A B C D E	125 A B C D E